UNSTOPPABLE

DAVE ANDERSON

UNSTOPPABLE

TRANSFORMING YOUR MINDSET

TO CREATE CHANGE,

ACCELERATE RESULTS,

AND BE THE BEST AT WHAT YOU DO

WILEY

Library of Congress Cataloging-in-Publication Data

Names: Anderson, Dave, author.
Title: Unstoppable : transforming your mindset to create change, accelerate
   results, and be the best at what you do / Dave Anderson.
Description: Hoboken, New Jersey : John Wiley & Sons, Inc., [2017] | Includes
   index. |
Identifiers: LCCN 2017023352 (print) | LCCN 2017036723 (ebook) | ISBN
   9781119412472 (pdf) | ISBN 9781119412496 (epub) | ISBN 9781119412434
   (cloth)
Subjects: LCSH: Employee motivation. | Organizational behavior. |
   Organizational change.
Classification: LCC HF5549.5.M63 (ebook) | LCC HF5549.5.M63 A59 2017 (print)
   | DDC 650.1–dc23
LC record available at https://lccn.loc.gov/2017023352

978-1-119-41243-4 (hardback)
978-1-119-41247-2 (ePDF)
978-1-119-41249-6 (ePUB)

Printed in the United States of America

SKY10024543_012821

Contents

Other Books by Dave Anderson

Unstoppable is dedicated to the late Alan Ram,
who lived a game changer life, and
contributed to this work shortly before his death.
Alan, your legend lives on.

Acknowledgments

Thirty-four very busy, highly accomplished men and women helped make this book possible, and certainly made it far better than I could have on my own. You will hear from them throughout the book. They represent a diverse field of experiences and expertise, all of which they share to help you become unstoppable. They answered my call to help, and selflessly set aside their own agendas to add value to you, the reader, and for that I am deeply grateful. You will be, too. They are:

Jim Afremow, PhD: Author, sports psychologist, and mental game coach

Samar Azem: Co-Head Coach, Campbell University women's soccer

Dan Barnette: Award-winning movie trailer editor

Brad Bartlett: President, Dole Packaged Foods NA/Europe

Ed Bastian: CEO, Delta Air Lines

Phil Beckner: Assistant Coach, Boise State University men's basketball

Doug Carter: Senior Vice President, EQUIP

Jeff Cowan: Sales trainer and CEO of Jeff Cowan's Pro Talk, Inc.

Tom Crean: Head college basketball coach and broadcaster

Scott Cross: Head Coach, University of Texas at Arlington men's basketball

Andrew Dettmann: Television producer and writer

Larry Dorfman: Chairman and CEO of EasyCare

Bjorn Englen: Rock star, legendary bass guitar player

Yogi Ferrell: Point guard, Dallas Mavericks

Robert Forrester: CEO, Vertu Motors PLC

Johnny Gyro: Seven-time Karate Champion, Owner at Johnny Gyro Karate

Adam Hermann: Director of Sports Performance, Boise State University

Jeff Janssen: Founder and President, Janssen Sports Leadership Center

Mike Klintworth: United States Air Force CMSgt., COO VETS, LLC

Meyers Leonard: Power forward, Portland Trail Blazers

Jason Loscalzo: Head Football Strength and Conditioning Coach, Washington State University

John Malishenko: COO, Germain Motor Company

Oliver Maroney: NBA insider and writer for *Dime* magazine

Allistair McCaw: Author, speaker, coach, and Director of McCaw Method Sports Performance

Shawn Meaike: President, Family First Life Insurance Company

Marisa Mills: Owner and CEO, Mills Automotive Group

Kevin Ozee: Director of Athletics, Arlington Independent School District

Cory Palka: Captain III—Hollywood Division, Los Angeles Police Department

Alan Ram: President and Founder, Alan Ram's Proactive Training Solutions

Whit Ramonat: Executive Vice President, Penske Automotive Group, Inc.

Eric Samuelson: President, Management Development Institute

Troy Tomlinson: President and CEO, Sony/ATV Nashville

David Williams: Vice President, Horizon Forest Products

Dave Wilson: CEO, Preston Automotive Group and iFrog Digital Marketing

A big thank you also goes to my LearnToLead team, particularly Ryan Cota, who, despite his other immense duties, served me with editing, suggesting, and formatting this manuscript from start to finish, and did it with complete excellence—just as he does everything else in his life. To my wife and partner Rhonda, and to my daughter and General Manager Ashley: Thanks for learning how to deal with me over the years as I am striving to meet a book deadline. Now on our fourteenth book together, I appreciate your support and flexibility to accommodate my quirks, demands, and obsessions throughout the process.

To the customers of LearnToLead in more than 30 countries, and to the supporters of our Matthew 25:35 Foundation, thank you for believing in and partnering with us, and for allowing our team to add value to your lives and organizations. It is our daily honor and privilege.

Let Us Hear from You

Throughout your reading of this book, let us hear from you! Send your photo with this book, your favorite quote, page number, and more on Twitter to @DaveAnderson100! Use the hashtag #Unstoppable.

Introduction

No birth certificate has ever proclaimed someone as "unstoppable." Nor has one ever declared someone "a sluggard," "mediocre," or "a pessimist." We become these not by declaration or genetics, but by our own decisions and grit (or lack thereof).

On an organization's roster, there are normally four types of team members: undertakers, caretakers, playmakers, and game changers. The behaviors associated with each category go beyond skills, knowledge, talent, or experience; they are primarily motivated by one's mindset. This in turn determines how well and consistently the skills, knowledge, talent, and experience of an individual are activated, thereby highly influencing his or her level of success. The following chapters will dig more deeply into each of the four categories, but for now, here is a brief introduction into each of the groups we will be discussing at length.

Undertakers

Undertakers bring a negative value to an organization. Two primary types of undertakers will be discussed in the first chapter; but know that the longer people perform at this level, the more damage they do to their own self-esteem, future, the culture, team morale, and results overall.

Caretakers

Caretakers are baseliners. More often than not, they do what is required of them and nothing more. They pledge allegiance to the status quo and to their job description. They do not initiate, bring new ideas, or offer solutions. If teammates are in trouble, you cannot depend on the caretaker to lift them up or carry their load. Caretakers often have the skills, knowledge, talent, and experience that would allow them to perform far above what they deliver; but, since they are not motivated to work that hard and are not interested in doing so, they drop anchor at the caretaker level.

Playmakers

Playmakers normally have more energy or drive than caretakers. They may also have more talent, but are primarily differentiated from caretakers in how their mindset enables them to apply their talent. They will occasionally do great things, but are not consistent enough to elevate their performance or results to reach game changer status. They are prone to letting the pat on the back become a massage, and their work ethic and urgency will fall as prosperity rises.

Game Changers

Game changers are unstoppable. They are relentless, which is defined as being "oppressively constant; incessant . . . unyielding" (Google 2017). These are the team members who consistently bring effort, energy, attitude, excellence, and passion to the job. It does not mean they always create the ideal outcome, but failure to do so is not due to lack of effort, energy, attitude, or work ethic.

It is important to understand two things up front about the four performance groups:

1. Everyone is normally a blend and spends some time in each group depending on his or her circumstances. However, one of the four mindsets will primarily dominate a person's time, which is then reflected in performance.

2. The groups are not permanent verdicts. As you will see, it is just as possible to think and perform as an undertaker and then become a game changer as it is to be on top, change your thinking and performance, and demote yourself to undertaker status.

In addition to discussing the four performance groups, *Unstoppable* will also outline steps to transform one's mindset from the lower groups upward, so that the game changer traits dominate your daily routine, your month, your year, and your life.

Perhaps the most exciting and helpful aspect of *Unstoppable* will be the insights from dozens of coaches, managers, CEOs, journalists, entrepreneurs, and elite performers into what separates the team member who occasionally makes things happen—the playmaker—from the person who far more consistently brings energy, focus, drive, passion, and excellence to a role—the unstoppable game changer.

For example, as the president and CEO of Sony/ATV Music publishing in Nashville, Troy Tomlinson works with some of the world's best-known playmaker and game changer status songwriters and artists. Tomlinson observes that the truly elite—the game changers—in his industry "possess a deep, focused passion for their art virtually every waking moment, and are willing to work harder than the hardest-working individual on their team" (Troy Tomlinson, pers. comm.). The same can be said for game changers in any field, anywhere.

Let me emphasize that you won't hear from passive, couch-potato performance theorists, but rather from in-the-trenches, been-there-and-done-that achievers and builders of people and organizations. Even better, the principles are so widely applicable that you should be able to relate to and apply them regardless of your field or experience level.

While talent is an essential contributor to optimal and consistently solid performance, it is often overhyped. And, while talent is a great head start to becoming unstoppable, at the end of the day it is only potential. Frankly, without a mindset that consistently and ferociously activates talent, performance disappointments reign.

As president of LearnToLead, I have averaged speaking 120 times annually across 17 countries for the past two decades, and one of my favorite questions to ask attendees in my game changer seminars is: "How many of you agree that the right mindset influences the ability to win, more than skills, knowledge, talent, or experience?" Droves of hands shoot up. I follow that question with this: "I agree. Now, since mindset is so important, how much time do you spend intentionally building yours each day?"

Crickets chirping

Time after time—blank stares, and total silence. A key objective of this book is to remedy this.

As the opening chapters outline common traits of each of the four performance groups, a common temptation is to begin thinking about other people and which group they most often fall into. While there is value in classifying others on your team in this manner, and then following up with subsequent coaching, the intent is for you to first assess *yourself* and upgrade *your own* mindset and performance; after all, you are more effective and credible when growing others after you have first prioritized growing yourself.

While reading a book or attending a course may create adrenaline and momentum, process and consistency bring change. To aid you in your personal development, I will also recommend various apps, websites, podcasts, online resources, and seminars to help you and those you care most about build a more robust game changer career and life. If your open mind, pen, and highlighter are ready to go, it's time to introduce you to the "undertaker."

CHAPTER 1

The Undertaker

One who daily does less than he can gradually becomes less than he is.

I won't devote much space to the undertaker performer. Frankly, who they are and what they do is as obvious as it is devastating. Here is a quick summary.

Undertakers Do Sub-Baseline Work

In the next chapter we will discuss the caretaker; and, while the caretaker at least does baseline work (not heroic by any means), the undertaker does not. Undertakers might be nice enough as people, but someone else continually has to carry their load, clean up their mess, or be frantically rushing around performing damage control in their wake. True to his or her classification, the undertaker undertakes and achieves nothing meaningful, and takes under or lowers morale, momentum, your brand, performance outcomes, cultural integrity, and your personal credibility. To exacerbate matters, the costs they inflict are not a one-time lump-sum payment. If only it were that simple! If only you could hold your nose one time, write a single check, and be done with the costs they inflict. But it is not that painless. For as long as you keep them, undertakers will create a torturous form of misery on the installment plan. The cost of keeping undertakers is staggering, and it can eventually put your organization on the endangered species list.

> **In essence, an undertaker is essentially unemployed, but still on your payroll. It is not the undertakers you remove from your organization that make you miserable; it's the ones you keep.**

Toxic Achievers Are Undertakers

Despite a cliché to the contrary, the fact is that you *can* argue with success, if someone is getting it at the cost of violating your values. While the first characterization of undertakers addressed the below-average performer, a toxic achiever is one who may perform well—he or she could even be a top performer—but who also violates your values, can be selfish and divisive, and creates ongoing drama that debilitates culture. Weak leaders tolerate toxic achievers because they produce, but in the process they relegate themselves to heartless, selfish, sellouts. The damage that undertaker toxic achievers do to your culture, credibility, and brand is incalculable. Undoubtedly, well-known undertakers may have come to mind as you read these words—high-profile athletes or hired guns in business who sojourn from team to team performing well and meanwhile poisoning the locker room. But if identifying others who may fit either of these two descriptions was your primary focus, then you have missed the point. While there is a recommended resource in the Appendix of this book to help you identify and develop game changers in your organization, the four performance groups in this book are not first and foremost about anyone else when you consider them; they are about you.

> **If you are lazy, selfish, or corrupt, you either won't use or will misuse your talent and make yourself completely expendable in the process.**

How often do you demonstrate the traits in either of the prior two points? How often do you become divisive, bitter, selfish, or territorial; do less than you can; or create messes that others must clean up? To reiterate what I mentioned earlier, we are normally all a blend of the four mindsets from time to time. But, to become unstoppable, it is essential we develop the mindset and focus to think and act as a game changer more consistently, so that it dominates our work and personal life.

"Everyone thinks of changing the world, but no one thinks of changing himself."—Leo Tolstoy (AZ Quotes 2017)

In my work consulting with retail clients like automotive dealers, I frequently observe sales representatives in both undertaker categories. On one hand there is "five-car Fred"—the underachiever—whom no one can count on to lift the team to a new level, and who predictably performs at substandard levels. But there's also "25-car Ted," who consistently leads the sales board, but thinks his high performance is a permission slip to live above the rules and values that the lesser performers are held accountable for. He comes in late, shortcuts processes, does not attend training, is not overly concerned about the rest of the team, and frequently conducts the "meeting after the meeting" at the watercooler to talk about how what was discussed by management is stupid, is irrelevant, or will never work.

If toxic achievers threaten to leave because they do not want to live your values, let them go. It's kind of like the trash taking itself out.

It's the Mindset

Incidentally, undertakers in both categories may be knowledgeable and highly skilled, possess impressive credentials, and be blessed with copious talent. But their mindset is seriously flawed, and all those aforementioned assets and advantages are never fully activated as a result. There are those who spend an inordinate amount of their personal and professional lives demonstrating undertaker characteristics who may be considered largely successful, but still miss their potential by miles.

No one individual can make another person an undertaker. Rather, undertakers cannot get out of their own way. They are products of their own poor decisions and excel in the art of self-destruction.

In summary, it is time to acknowledge where your self-destructive mindsets and actions have sabotaged your personal and professional life, and renounce those things immediately. You can change them. No one else but *you* can. It is not acceptable to do less than you are able. There is no way that is okay.

Nor is it tolerable to do great work but think you are above the values and behaviors that others must adhere to. In fact, that demonstrates an arrogance and selfishness that is disgusting. The great news is that you can change all of this—not by waiting for someone else to change or for something to change, but by changing your thinking. Life is short. Wake up. You cannot afford to spend one more minute living or working like an undertaker. You can and must do better.

There are three stages of accountability in organizations. Stage one is top-down, which is the most common and weakest. Stage two is peer-to-peer accountability, which is a step up and creates a stronger culture. Stage three is self-accountability, which is where game changers reside ("I do it because I said I would"). Undertakers make stage one their homestead.

Mission Unstoppable

To become an unstoppable game changer, you must master the following mindset and behavioral adjustments:

1. Don't even think about doing work that is less in quality or quantity than your absolute best. If you want to know how a game changer answers the question "How much is enough?," the answer is simple: "All I possibly can."

   The good news for those aspiring to stand out in any organization is that it is not crowded at the top; it is crowded at the bottom. There is intense competition among the mediocre, where the undertakers and caretakers work and live. The recipe for standing out in a positive manner is both basic and brilliantly concise: Do all you can—the best you can—and do it every time.

   David Williams, vice president of Horizon Forest Products, says:

   > Game changers are the best at what they do. They are the ones who are always at the top of the lists in regard to success in the company. They make up less than 10 percent of those in their position, not only in your company but in the industry.
   >
   > They will simply outwork everyone else. They will be the ones that are in early and stay late. They do not work according to a clock or a time schedule. They will do whatever it takes to *win*, and they know that it does not happen in an eight-hour day. When you find these game changers, pay them well and do whatever you have to do to keep them on the team. They are successful people who will be a huge part of the success of the team. You absolutely need these people, so find a way to keep these people on your team. (David Williams, pers. comm.)

   And Williams should know. He took over Horizon Forest Products, a wholesale flooring distributor, 19 years ago as it was ready to go out of business, and guided its turnaround. It is now one of the largest distributors in the industry, and one of the most profitable; and it didn't happen with a team that arrived at 8:59 and left at 5:01.

2. If you are a top performer, stay humble and know that you are not above values and rules, and that what is good for the team will not be subordinated to your personal pride, preferences, or comfort zone.

   In other words, it is not all about you. So get over yourself (everyone else has), and expect to be measured by two metrics: performance and behavioral excellence—and know that excelling at the former does not excuse neglect of the latter.

3. As mentioned in the Introduction, it is important to remember that undertaker tendencies are not permanent verdicts for you or others; but to facilitate movement to more productive groups, a change in mindset will be required.

4. Use additional and helpful resources to help yourself and others create game changer performance. For daily quotes, tips, and strategies, follow us on Twitter: @DaveAnderson100 and @LearntoLead100.

Heads up to top performers—we love you, but you are not the center of the universe. That job has already been taken. You are not bigger than the team.

CHAPTER 2

The Caretaker

*So you also, when you have done everything you were told to do, should
say, "We are unworthy servants; we have only done our duty."*
—Luke 17:10 (Biblica 2017)

The caretaker is a "just enough" performer. He does just enough
to get by, just enough to get paid, and just enough to not get fired.
While caretaker performance is a step up from the unacceptable
undertaker, it is not noble; in fact, it is not even particularly notable. It
is baseline, minimal, get-in-at-the-last-minute, leave-at-the-earliest-
moment, pledge-allegiance-to-the-job-description, just-hold-it-all-
together-while-you're-there performance.

For a caretaker, the thought of putting in extra work and effort to
become his or her best self, or to get an edge and move ahead, is as
appealing as a dead skunk in the middle of the road.

Do not complain about the success you don't get from
the work you will not do. If you did not earn it and do
not deserve it, you have earned and deserve the reality
of going without it.

The Caretaker Antithesis

Phil Beckner is a men's assistant basketball coach at Boise State University and has an extended history coaching Portland Trail Blazer Damian Lillard, dating back to Lillard's time at Weber State. Beckner continues to serve as a personal coach and mentor, and trains Lillard now in two-week stints during off-seasons. Lillard has a world-class work ethic that he has developed over the years, which has lifted him to game changer status in the National Basketball Association (NBA), but it started well before he turned pro. Coach Beckner observes:

> One of the most relentless and driven competitors . . . tireless, freak workers I have ever been around is Damian Lillard. You can easily identify Lillard as a game changer because of the impact he has had on the people and teams he has been a part of. Early on, Dame had a *healthy fear*; . . . he wouldn't accept not improving; he refused to become comfortable; he refused to become complacent; . . . he didn't rest on his past accomplishments. He worked hard. Period.
>
> After his first season in the NBA and being named NBA rookie of the year, Lillard trained with the same inner circle of people he worked with the previous summer, but Lillard would still grow scared. Not scared to compete. Not scared to go up against the best of the best in the NBA at the best position in the NBA (point guard), but scared that he would not improve enough. Scared that he couldn't evolve. Scared that every other point guard in the NBA was possibly working harder, and trying to get better than him. So he used the same formula he always did—the same formula other game changers use. He worked harder, and harder, and harder. He lifted more, he trained more, he shot more, and he watched more video (Phil Beckner, pers. comm.).

For an undertaker or caretaker to shift into becoming a Damian Lillard, it does not take an additional smidgen of talent. It does, however, require a seismic shift in mindset; which, by the way, *you* are in control of changing. This also means you are to blame if you do not change it.

To be capable of doing more, but then to make a conscious choice not to, is just a sneakier, more creative way of quitting.

Drop the Excuses

What is worse than choosing to do less than you can is the reasoning that some use to justify their own caretaker performance, or the mediocrity of others:

"I do what I'm supposed to do. I do my job."
"I'll do more when they pay me more."
"My boss/coach doesn't motivate me."
"At least I'm here every day."
"He's not great, but he's better than nothing."
"Well, she is at least reliable."
"I've seen worse."

This stinking thinking is the lament of losers—the verbal vomit known as excuses. Excuses are the DNA of underachievers, and pretty much guarantee that you will spend a lot of your work life, and life overall, in caretaker status. Excuses are just a plea offered to explain away a fault or failure. They are an absolution of responsibility. Excuses make you common, undesirable, and ultimately average, ordinary, and not outstanding. If I may be so blunt, they also make you repulsive. No one wants to be around someone who makes excuses—*NO ONE*.

Johnny Gyro is my karate instructor and has trained me to the rank of second-degree black belt. Master Gyro is a ninth-degree black belt in Tang Soo Do karate who has trained in the martial arts for five decades. He dominated the 1980s as its top-ranked fighter, is in martial arts halls of fame, holds black belts in five additional martial arts, and has been an instructor for more than three decades training and developing hundreds of black belts. Master Gyro was a member of the United States Fight Team for six years, and its captain for three years. His 29-time winning record of the annual International Karate Championship stands in a league of its own. This unstoppable game changer decided early on that excuses were the language of mediocrity—a futile exercise he wouldn't stoop to engage in. That decision was a catalyst in separating him from the hordes of caretakers in his field, and in elevating him to the eventual status of game changer.

From the start, I refused to waste my time making any excuses for myself and I rejected the option to fall victim to useless "reasons" why I didn't win a fight if I lost. Instead, I remained fixated on focusing on my direction. I always had my target in sight. It was always on my mind and I kept that tunnel vision in the forefront of my thoughts to keep my drive alive on what I planned to achieve. It didn't matter who I fought or where I fought because I competed across the USA and through Canada, Mexico, and Central America. A second-place victory was not a victory in my mind. While some gifted karate fighters considered second place a win, I did not because, in my mind, first place was the only win that mattered. Anything less was merely participating in a fight, because coming in second wasn't going to get me where I needed to go. I was not willing to settle for second best, and knowing there were no shortcuts was fine with me. I wanted to earn my titles because I wasn't interested in finding ways around that. I went about learning how other tough fighters trained, how they prepared for the ring. If a winning fighter trained by doing 500 kicks a day with ankle weights on, I did 1,000 kicks with ankle weights. Fighting was as much a mental game as a physical game. Strategy mattered, knowledge mattered, and I learned how to become a smart fighter. Physical training can only take you so far. The mind drives the desire and the body follows. The true definition of a fighter is one who understands his challenge and knows how to simultaneously train the mind and the body to conquer the challenge (Johnny Gyro, pers. comm.).

To change your results, change your behaviors. To change your behaviors, change your thinking. To change your thinking, change what you think about. To think about the right things, renounce excuses and focus on what you can control.

Seven Caretaker Symptoms

So how much of your day, week, month, year, or life do you spend in maintenance mode—in caretaker status? Here are seven symptoms to help you identify and correct the mindsets, habits, and behaviors that are causing you to miss your best possible life while on the job, and away from it.

1. In caretaker status you will excel at finding problems without offering solutions. You add little value to current situations. Instead, you just "hold down the fort." A game changer, on the other hand, is a value adder.
Jeff Cowan's Pro Talk is a 29-year-old premier training company in automotive-related fields that over three decades has served 3,000 clients. A key principle that Cowan's training teaches not only his own team, but his clients as well, is to leave situations better than you found them. Cowan notes:

   > A game changer is someone who makes significant contributions to an existing situation, sometimes so much so that a transformation takes place and a new norm is established. One of my main objectives when searching for a new hire is to identify an individual who possesses a skill set that will enable him or her to infuse something new and innovative into our existing business culture. In short, I *only* look for and bring in new team members that I

believe have the potential to be game changers. These are people who demonstrate that they have the desire and ability to elevate themselves and our company. Our hiring process is extensive and comprehensive and I take great pride in acknowledging that to date I have been extremely successful in fulfilling that goal (Jeff Cowan, pers. comm.).

Caretakers point out problems like there is a reward for it. Game changers point out problems as well, but offer solutions to remedy and fix them, and move forward.

2. Whereas game changers measure their impact by how high they lift others, when you are in caretaker status you will be so wrapped up in yourself that you will not have time to help or elevate teammates.

   The legendary Bill Russell is an 11-time NBA champion, five-time MVP, and 12-time all-star. Despite his immense personal accomplishments, his philosophy on impacting teammates is a mindset that caretakers—and even most playmakers—do not understand, value, or aspire to: "The most important measure of how good a game I played is how much better I'd made my teammates play" (Bill Russell, AZ Quotes 2017). That brings up a couple of important questions: How much better do your teammates play because you are working with them? Does the impact you have on teammates—for better or for worse—even matter to you?

You don't have a neutral impact on your team. You are either adding value or subtracting value by default. Doing less than you can do subtracts value.

3. When in caretaker status, you will not initiate or risk, but will instead tweak, react, maintain, defend, entrench, and pledge allegiance to tradition, old times' sake, and sentimentalism. Game

changers attack the status quo, and when things do not turn out as planned, they never look at failure as fatal.

Allistair McCaw, of McCaw Method Sports Performance, is recognized as a world leader in the field of sports performance and athlete development. The author of 7 *Keys to Being a Great Coach*, he has worked with an array of top sports stars, including tennis player and former Women's Tennis Association World No. 1 ranked Dinara Safina, two-time Grand Slam Champion Svetlana Kuznetsova of Russia, current Olympic gold medalist Monica Puig, two World No. 1 ranked men's and women's squash players (Ramy Ashour and Nicol David), and many more.

In Coach McCaw's observation, top performers initiate and take risks because even in failure they become better: "Game changers love to compete and are fueled by the thrill and challenge of testing themselves every time they step out to perform. These performers have a growth mindset, meaning they are not afraid to fail or take risks. They see failure only as a better way to learn and do better next time" (Allistair McCaw, pers. comm.).

If everything you do is a matter of life or death, you are going to be dead a lot. When game changers hit a wall, they bounce; they do not splatter. This makes them unstoppable.

---

4. When in caretaker status, you will lack having a standard for yourself that is so high that it would require you to show up, be your best, and prove yourself over again each day. Instead you will require excessive amounts of external motivation to perform at better-than-expected levels; and often, you will need to be given a deadline, a financial incentive, or a threat to trigger above-average urgency.

Sony/ATV Music's Troy Tomlinson makes this insightful observation:

> In music, elite performers aren't on a field competing against another team. What makes them elite is that they

play against themselves. They play to improve themselves. Self-awareness is big here. They're in a constant state of self-examination, and to do that you have to be aware there's a need to examine and improve. This is what the elite do; they constantly examine how they can make it better. This drives and motivates them. If it's about the money, there'll never be enough money. Many artists died before their works sold for money. They don't do it for the money; they can't help but do it (Troy Tomlinson, pers. comm.).

On the other hand, lazy caretakers act as though they cannot help but *not* do it. Their laziness is a subtle form of theft. It steals from their family, employer, teammates, and society, and robs them of their own best future. If the idea of associating caretaker performance and laziness seems harsh, consider the definition of lazy: "unwilling to work or use energy" (Google 2017). *That* is the caretaker in six simple words.

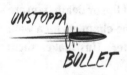

No one has the time or energy to hit you in the head with a bat every day and drag you around the bases. Your leader and peers would much rather have to calm down a geyser than motivate a mudhole.

5. When in caretaker status, you are known more for reacting and playing catch-up, rather than for being the team's go-to person— the game changer whom others turn to when they need action that brings predictable results.

Captain Cory Palka is the CEO equivalent for the Hollywood Division of the Los Angeles Police Department (LAPD). A 30-year-plus veteran of the force with 350 officers under his command, he has seen his share of performers from all four groups, in all geographical bureaus of the city, during the course of his career. Speaking about one of his go-to game changers in Hollywood, Sergeant Neil Wank, Palka remarked:

Neil is engaged. Whether it be in the field, on roll call, or in the station house, he is always engaged. His thirst for knowledge of policy and retention of that LAPD policy is top-notch.

Neil was raised in Brooklyn, New York, with a father who was a mechanic at a local auto shop. He [Neil] has a work ethic of "excellence always" and never leaves anything on the table. He does not see life that way. He plays chess while others play checkers. He has the understanding of managerial expectations, yet he can relate to the needs of subordinate street cops while balancing expectations of myself and the needs of the community.

At a recent Academy Awards ceremony, Neil was the deputy to the captain assigned to the Exterior Branch of the Incident Command System. He reported to me, as I had specifically asked he be assigned that role. He was my main "fireman" who put out issue after issue after issue. As I was fed information about protest groups along the limo route leading into the Dolby Theatre, Neil was not only physically present to brief me on the status of the groups, but he held the vision to know where any strengths lay within those groups to disrupt the show or become a distraction to the show. Groups such as Dakota Pipeline Protest group, Westboro Baptist Church group, Chinese for Human Rights group, City of LA Workers Union, and Pro-President Trump group were all present. Neil ensured that each group was provided a route, direction, time, and place that would not conflict with the others. He offered no complaints or excuses in the heat of battle; he just got it done.

When the show's producers complained about other police agencies being on the red carpet and taking photos during inappropriate times, it was Neil who, without delay, put out the fire and firmly instructed the California Highway Patrol captain, lieutenant, and offending officers to stop their behavior.

Neil's men will follow him through a wall, as he cares deeply for their interests while protecting the interests of the command, community, and politicians (Cory Palka, pers. comm.).

One who has developed a reputation for getting things done right and fast will never want for more opportunities, influence, or empowerment.

6. When in caretaker status, you are not committed to prepare or to improve your skill set, mindset, or organization. You are pretty much in it for yourself, and your attitude is to just do your job, and you do it pretty much like you are serving a prison sentence.

Bjorn Englen is one of the world's foremost bass guitar players. He has played bass for Yngwie Malmsteen, Billboard #1 Quiet Riot, and Scorpions guitarist Uli Jon Roth, and currently plays in Soul Sign, in Dio's official band Dio Disciples, and with Tony MacAlpine.

Note, as Bjorn describes his game changer, Mike, how many of the traits mentioned in this chapter are being lived out, and how Mike is the antithesis of a caretaker. We all need a Mike, and to learn to be more like Mike.

> When I think of a game changer, I think of three traits: commitment, loyalty, and enthusiasm. Someone who immediately comes to mind is a musician whom I hired to play in my own group Soul Sign a few years ago. I had been struggling with various "hired gun" players for years and often focused on getting name players into the band. This didn't seem to do the trick, as most of them (although good friends and talented) often lacked one or more of the above-mentioned qualities (commitment, loyalty, and/or enthusiasm). Most of them are great friends and incredible musicians, but often turned out to be talented "playmakers." I soon realized that a paid fee per show or

rehearsal often didn't trigger any of the traits I was most looking for. Instead, getting someone to be a member of the band to share profits, expenses, and decisions seemed to be a much more beneficial and effective approach.

When I suggested to Mike to come and audition for the band, I gave him three songs off the latest CD to learn. He replied, "I already know the whole album." He drove for more than two hours to the audition and showed up 45 minutes early. During the audition, he stopped playing in the middle of two different songs to correct me and the others about the song arrangement! We were, to say the least, both very impressed and happy. Since then I have mentioned to several people how Mike gave himself the job. He basically didn't give us any reason to turn him down. Following the audition, we rehearsed once or twice a week for about 18 months. Mike would drive 140 miles each way and was never once late. He would always show up in a good mood with a big smile on his face and would always insist on working hard with very few short breaks. He would never complain about money or expenses, but instead he would be proactive and talk about how we could improve our performances, get more bookings, etc. Needless to say, he became my right arm. His loyalty was to the band, and to me as a leader and founder of the group, and he would often speak for me to other members of the group to get them to follow rules or plans that were set and agreed upon. Mike turned out to be a true game changer, and he set an example for what kind of team members we should be looking for in order to reach great success (Bjorn Englen, pers. comm.).

While caretakers limp through the first mile whining the whole way, game changers traverse the second, third, and beyond—not because they have to, but because they want to.

7. When in caretaker status, you will not seek feedback about how you can improve; and, when someone offers it, you respond as though you are about to be choked out by Connor McGregor. You also tend to take it personally and would rather pout than improve. Or you listen to it and may even agree with it, but you change nothing because of it. You are just too comfortable with how things are to engage in the discomfort of progress. You accept things because they are familiar, not because they are the best. As a result, you do not grow; you plateau. Oppositely, game changers not only act on feedback they receive, but they seek it out and insist on it. Germain Automotive Group is a 70-year-old company that has 15 franchises across three states. They sell upwards of 25,000 vehicles annually and give broad autonomy to the general managers of each entity. John Malishenko, the COO and a two-decade team member of Germain, explains how acceptance of coaching and feedback is a key growth catalyst for his management team: "When I look at our leadership team and think about what, beyond talent, makes them special, it's their adaptability and willingness to embrace change that make them 'game changers.' While they all have a degree of dominance, it seems to be their humility or not needing to be right that allows them to improve continuously. They welcome constructive criticism and don't get defensive or take it personally" (John Malishenko, pers. comm.).

UNSTOPPA
BULLET

The caretaker performer is more committed to being comfortable than to getting better. Game changers, in contrast, listen to the feedback from those who know them best. They know it is better to be humbled by them than to be humiliated before the masses.

In summary, caretaker performers in any realm are common, nothing special, easy to find, and cheap to keep. Whatever caretaker trait resonated with you—or made you the most uncomfortable—may also have the most to teach you about where you have let up and are declining both personally and professionally.

Being mediocre is not okay. You were not created to be mediocre. Mediocre is defined as "average or ordinary" (Dictionary.com 2017)—not outstanding. Mediocre thinking evokes mediocre behaviors and effort, which in turn create mediocre results, lulling you down the path to a mediocre life. Mediocre lives are sad: People die at 40 but are not buried until they are 80. You have the opportunities, talents, and drive to be far more than average, or you would not have bought, opened, or made it this far in the book. The important point for you at this moment is to ask yourself, "Where am I no longer willing to sell myself short, let myself and others down, and give less than my best?" The exercises in Mission Unstoppable will help you to answer this and to turn good intentions into meaningful action.

Mission Unstoppable

To become an unstoppable game changer, evaluate and act on the following four key points:

1. Based on the comparisons given in this chapter between a caretaker mindset and performance and a game changer mindset and performance, evaluate your own performance with brutal honesty (lying to yourself is a recipe for eventual irrelevance).
   - What percentage of your daily routine, your week, your month, and your year is spent thinking and acting like a caretaker versus a game changer?
   - Do you "turn it on" only when time is running out or your back is against the wall? What would be the impact of "turning it on" 10, 20, 30, 100 percent more, over the course of a lifetime?
2. Considering the percentage of your time spent in caretaker status, reevaluate some of the key traits of game changers contributed by other game changers in this chapter, and identify those you must embrace and act on daily (and every day means every day—EDMED).

- Maintains a healthy fear of *not* improving, remaining the same, and being left behind.
- Renounces excuses for doing less than he can, and being less than his best.
- Adds value to situations and is obsessed with solutions, not with problems.
- Possesses an awareness and concern for how his attitude, work ethic, and performance impact teammates.
- Makes changes, takes risks, and considers subsequent disappointments or setbacks as a chance to learn and improve.
- Competes more with his or her own self than with others. Retains a continual focus to better one's former best in order to ultimately become *the* best.
- Builds a reputation as the go-to person on a team who gets results without excuses or delay, and is the clutch teammate who knows how to deliver and how to win.
- Consistently prepares him- or herself, and brings daily enthusiasm and a contagious commitment that sets the tone for the team.

3. No one has a neutral impact on the team. You are either elevating it or diminishing it in some way, every day. Which impact are you causing? Whatever mindsets, habits, or character flaws are holding you back must be replaced with something more productive.

4. Use additional and helpful resources to help yourself and others create game changer performance. Join the free Insider Club at www.LearnToLead.com for hundreds of free articles and videos on personal development, sales, leadership, and more.

There comes a time when you have to give up what is holding you back so you can go up, grow up, and discover your potential.

CHAPTER 3

The Playmaker

Good, great, and elite performers do similar things. What often separates one group from the others is the consistency and excellence with which they do them.

Whereas an undertaker mindset and performance are unacceptable, and a caretaker's are mediocre, a playmaker demonstrates a significant upgrade in mindset, energy, drive, and performance. Consider the playmaker somewhat of a "game changer light"—doing many of the right things and demonstrating the same resilient mindset, just not nearly as consistently as the game changer (for reasons this chapter will begin to explain—and they are all fixable).

A Vital Role

It is unlikely you will have a team or be on a team with nothing but game changers. Thus, playmakers play a vital role on any team. With mindset adjustments that evoke more consistent and productive behaviors, playmakers can elevate themselves to the status of game changer among their teammates. Remember, it is not a difference just in physical effort, but in mental strength, that is a key separator between playmakers and game changers.

Automotive and banking executive Dave Wilson Sr. explains his own evolution in this regard. But first, for perspective, here is a short background on this game-changing entrepreneur. Preston Ford Inc. was founded in 1975. Becoming a partner in 1981, Dave Wilson Sr. later bought out the original founder in 1992. Preston Ford has since evolved into the Preston Automotive Group with 13 locations representing nine brands. Preston Ford has been in Ford's Top 100 dealers over the years, ranking number 63 in the nation out of 3,200 Ford dealers in 2016. This prestigious distinction has gained nationwide attention due to the population of the town out of which Preston Ford operates (Preston, Maryland), which has a population of just over 700 people. The Preston Automotive Group has been recognized by all of the brands it represents for superior customer satisfaction and high sales efficiency. In 2014 Dave Wilson Sr. founded iFrog Digital Marketing, which services dealers found across the United States by managing all of their digital marketing needs. Wilson is also chairman of the board of Provident State Bank. In his own words:

> The biggest difference between a playmaker and a game changer is that a playmaker celebrates after every win. When this happens, they lose focus of the long-term goal and get out of their zone.
>
> The game changer, on the other hand, puts a check mark beside the accomplishment and looks for ways to keep moving his or her team forward to maximize results.
>
> In my career, I have been the playmaker and the game changer. Early on as the playmaker, everything was about "I" and very little was about "we." I would run around and put out fires and not teach my leaders what I did. Once everything was fixed, I would move on to the next problem, only to look over my shoulder and see that the fire was starting up again behind me.
>
> I soon learned that I couldn't fix the problem, celebrate the win, and move on. I had to mentor my leaders and hold them

accountable for our mutually desired results. Being the play-maker is like an addiction—getting high off the win and losing focus on the big picture.

As a game changer, the biggest win for me is watching my leaders win. We recently were recognized by Ford Motor Company for being one of the Top 100 Dealers in the country. My son and I attended this event together. Right before they called our names, I looked over to my son and told him he was going to receive the award for us. He said, "No, they are going to call your name." He's a Jr., so I thought it would be very easy for him to step in. He kept pushing back, so I had to take the recognition.

When walking out of the event, I told him that this would never happen again, saying, "Next time, it is all yours—you and your team won this coveted award! This will never repeat itself." He conceded and gave me his word that it would never happen again.

Later, as we both went to our rooms, I smiled to myself and realized how much I had grown over the years. I had become a game changer rather than a playmaker! I had moved from "I" to "we"—from "we" to a much better place! I don't need to take credit for anything. This feeling was and is so very heart-warming and gratifying. As a game changer you don't need the recognition; your real self-satisfaction is when your team maximizes its results and sets its sights on raising the bar even higher, as my son does as a result of my example.

You will have playmakers on your team. The key to leading them is keeping them in the zone and celebrating their wins with them, but also making sure that when the win happens, they don't *ever* think they have arrived and let complacency set in. In our organization, we say all of the time that "Compla-cency Kills," and trust me, it does. A game changer is a leader who can harness playmakers, keep them focused, and win every day. The vision is clear for the game changer. When this happens, the playmaker becomes very close to a game changer and doesn't even know it. This is when you will see a dramatic shift in your culture for the better. Your team will become focused on a collective vision and team members will believe in their hearts that it can and will be accomplished through hard work and perseverance (Dave Wilson, pers. comm.).

 **The first steps in moving from playmaker to unstoppable game changer status start with decisions, not conditions.**

Family First Life is one of the most dynamic and fastest-growing insurance enterprises in the United States, and the number-one distributor of Mutual of Omaha insurance. Family First Life's president, Shawn Meaike, has an energy and a passion for business and life that set the tone for the rest of the company. Meaike describes a key difference in mindset between playmakers and game changers as follows:

In my experience, the following attributes separate the "playmaker" from the "game changer." The game changer consistently demonstrates strength all day, every day. Let me give you an example; I have a vice president, Michael, who is based in Atlanta and manages a team of over 250 people. Earlier this year, Michael was going through an extremely difficult time professionally where his business could have really suffered, but you would never have known it! Game changers don't display fear, weakness, trepidation, or ambivalence; they charge forward and inspire others to do the same. Michael increased his volume over 50 percent in three months while dealing with the biggest professional struggles he had ever faced. The key to his success was that *none* of his team members knew he was going through a difficult time. Game changers never look for others to tell them it is going to be okay; they are a rock of strength that keeps people intense every day (Shawn Meaike, pers. comm.).

When most people have a bad day, everyone knows it. It shows in body language and attitude. When a game changer has a less than good day he or she sucks it up and bears it; game changers do not put strife on their sleeves and wear it.

Three Key Differentiators

In addition to differences in their levels of consistency, playmakers and game changers differ in other notable areas. Since there are too many to mention in a single chapter, I will focus on three:

1. **The playmaker has a greater need for external motivation than the game changer.** A playmaker is motivated more by external forces, and craves personal glory, excessive affirmation, and credit. When he or she does not get it, the person tends to pout and let up.

   To game changers, recognition is nice but is not necessary. They are their own harshest critics and have higher expectations for themselves than anyone else could have for them. They are much more intrinsically motivated. So for them, the pat on the back is great, but in their minds they say, "I'd have done it anyway, because that's how I'm wired."

   Samar Azem grew up in Africa and moved to the United States 14 years ago when she came to study and play soccer. She played at Campbell University and is now their co-head coach for women's soccer. In the past 10 years, she has coached in more than 210 games and has been part of three championships as both a player and a coach. In Coach Azem's view:

   > The playmakers as you've defined them encompass what as a coach I would perceive as a comfortable athlete. This person likely has a fixed mindset. They are unable to cross a threshold of mediocrity due to contentment with their current state or ability. These are typically the athletes

that are externally motivated, and the effect of that rare spike in performance, though minimal, typically comes from an external variable (avoidance of punishment, drive for reward, etc.).

In my experiences, the athletes that are defined as your "game changers"—that bring intensity day in and day out—are usually intrinsically motivated, even though it is unrealistic to think an individual can always bring "100 percent." Even the greatest athletes often struggle to be 100 percent, 100 percent of the time.

However, more times than not, the game changer is bringing a consistently high level of energy and drive. The separating attribute between the playmaker and the game changer, as you've described them, is the extrinsic versus intrinsic motivation in those athletes (Samar Azem, pers. comm.).

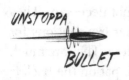

Playmakers snorkel at the surface of greatness but never plunge into the deep dive of consistent sacrifice. Nor do they tap the power of intrinsic motivation that would eventually make them unstoppable.

2. **The playmaker is more "me" centered and selfish than the game changer, who is generally humbler and has a stronger team concept.** To that end, a playmaker isn't overly concerned when a team member is struggling. This is because, in a sense, another's tough stretch makes the playmaker look better, and shines a brighter light on his or her performance. A game changer, on the other hand, competes more against him- or herself than with others, and is more global in concern for the elevation of all team members to a higher level.

Arlington, Texas, is a region that is rich in competitive sports and is demanding of high performance, traditionally beginning in grade school and continuing on to professional teams like the Texas Rangers and Dallas Cowboys. Kevin Ozee, director of athletics for the Arlington Independent School District, notes, "Interestingly enough, the game changers that I have met have very low egos. Many of them are introverts. They are more concerned about improving their game with a sense of humility instead of the 'look at me' syndrome that we see so much today. Game changers put the team's need before their own needs. Game changers manage their focus more than managing their time" (Kevin Ozee, pers. comm.).

> The game changer doesn't think less of him- or herself than the playmaker. They just think of themselves less and of teammates more than the playmaker does.

Tom Crean coached the Indiana University men's basketball team for nine years. Renowned for his recruiting and player-development ability, Coach Crean has prepared men like Dwyane Wade, Steve Novak, Cody Zeller, Travis Diener, Victor Oladipo, Wesley Matthews, Noah Vonleh, Jordan Hulls, Christian Watford, Troy Williams, Yogi Ferrell, and more for careers beyond basketball at the college level. When describing the transformation of Yogi Ferrell, the Indiana University all-time assist leader, Crean observes: "There came a time in his senior year, when we came from 16 points behind to beat Notre Dame, when Yogi stopped trying to prove how good he was, and just realized how good he was, and allowed it to come out. When that transformation happens, a player realizes he is going to start to need the rest of his teammates more, and will help make them better. He understood the entire team had to flourish for us to get where we wanted to go" (Tom Crean, pers. comm.).

3. **The playmaker strives for the extraordinary. The game changer focuses on doing the ordinary extraordinarily well.** Because the playmaker loves the spotlight, he or she strives toward the spectacular. Not that doing so is a bad thing, but is it the best thing? The game changer believes that by becoming brilliant in the basics, and mastering the ordinary things that most

others overlook or shortcut, he or she will become extraordinary in the process.

The head football strength and conditioning coach at Washington State University, Jason Loscalzo, has had the unique privilege of training and grooming hordes of athletes over the years, some of whom attain game changer status. His observations on their attention to detail explain this third point well. Get your highlighter ready, because these insights are laced with pure gold:

> In my opinion, being a game changer is not about being extraordinary; rather, it requires the ability, drive, and motivation to do the ordinary better than the next person or the competition. They realize that games and competition are won by seizing the opportunity at hand. They don't wait for the right moment; instead they make the moment count. This trait creates consistency in effort and mindset. There is a reason why game changers never get bored with the mundane everyday basic tasks to stay sharp and ready. If you were to walk into any practice for college or National Football League (NFL) football teams, any boardroom in Fortune 500 companies, or any successful small business, you would be able to identify the game changers simply by watching how they practice the required basics of their craft. They are very detail orientated in even the most basic requirements. They are relentless at always challenging themselves and improving the mundane tasks. They realize that preparation is the key to success and that preparation is all that you need to be ready for the game-changing moment.
>
> It comes in the form of having a detail-oriented approach to the simple everyday tasks. When watching athletes train, one can pick out game changers simply by observing the body language and effort given to warm-ups, basic movement skill, and basic lifting techniques. Game changers are those who put the same energy, effort, and

competitiveness into the ordinary as they do the energy, effort, and competitiveness in the fourth quarter of a tight game.

The old adage that "big-time players make big-time plays in big-time games" is misleading and downright false. Big-time players make the plays that count in crucial moments because they make routine plays when others around them are caught up in the moment. Game changers are able to make those routine plays simply because they have prepared themselves to do so through practicing the ordinary so much that it not only becomes second nature, but it's what they compete at daily to improve. Their focus and intensely competitive nature draw them to performing at a high level all the time, not just in crucial situations. They happen to shine because they are perceived as being able to make extraordinary things happen when perception is focused solely on one defining moment. If perception were based on the game changer's everyday focus, there would be no extraordinary perception; instead it would be what is expected from an individual who trains for perfecting the ordinary.

Even the everyday ordinary is an opportunity to compete. The Navy SEAL saying, "In times of pressure you don't rise to the occasion; you fall to your level of training," is the mantra for all game changers whether they be elite military, Fortune 500, or part of a sports team. As the pressure mounts in any situation, the game changer is able to rely on and trust in his or her ability to perform because *the focus is not on the moment or any possible outcome, but on his or her responsibility, leadership, and task.*

I have come across many athletes in my coaching career who fit this mold, but two of the most talented individuals in terms of being game changers by doing ordinary tasks better than their competition were both Boston College players—Matt Ryan and Luke Kuechly. Both men were absolute masters of their craft (practice and preparation) and relentless practice players. Their ability to prepare was uncanny due to one simple trait—they lived the process of preparation. They were two of the calmest individuals in the locker room on game day simply because their mindset and focus weren't on the moment itself, but on their responsibility for leadership and execution of ordinary tasks. And that calmness came because they spent their entire careers preparing for those moments. Practice wasn't different from games. Practice and games were both opportunities to improve their craft and leadership ability. Off-season workouts were no different than games or practice. They worked, and worked, and worked to fix and improve the little things and the tiniest of flaws that we saw as coaches and that they perceived as weak points in their game.

One particular game at Boston College for Matt Ryan sums up his ability to focus on the ordinary routine tasks in pressure situations. On October 25, 2007, Boston College visited Virginia Tech in a Thursday night showdown with national implications. Both teams were at the top of their respected divisions in the ACC and both were top 10 teams (#2 BC vs. #8 VT). The weather that late October night was awful, to say the least, with heavy rain and wind. Through the first three and a half quarters of that game, it was a pure defensive battle with both offenses struggling not only due to the weather, but also due to brilliant defense play and coaching for both teams. We were down 10–0 with a little more than 3:00 left in the game. All night we had sputtered on offense and made little progress; however, on this drive Matt was finally able to get something working, and we scored to make it 10–7 with 2:11 left. We then executed a perfect onside kick, recovering the ball for one final shot at winning or at least a tie for overtime. I can remember looking over to where Matt was on the sideline and there was zero panic or nerves. He was simply rehearsing what our next drive would need to be in order to be successful. The ensuing drive saw Matt having to improvise and execute under immense pressure from a tremendous Virginia Tech front that created all kinds of problems for us. However, that is when he was able to shine, not because he was suddenly able to do extraordinary things, but because these were the very situations he practiced, visualized, and prepared for on a daily basis, year-round. With 11 seconds left Matt was able to scramble away from pressure, find time, and then find a wide-open receiver in the back of the end zone for the game-winning 24-yard touchdown pass. It was his ability to focus on making routine plays, not pressing or trying to do too much, that made him successful in that perceived pressure position. Although it took a team of coaches and players on those two drives in under 3:00 to win a huge game on the road, it takes key players making game-changing execution the norm when others around them are looking for leadership. His calm and routine play mindset not only focused him for the task at hand in that situation, but it focused an entire team to work together and execute the ordinary everyday practiced techniques and game plan.

Luke Kuechly was a 17-year-old freshman linebacker out of St. Xavier High School in Cincinnati, Ohio, in June of 2009 when he stepped on campus at Boston College. That summer training cycle he would have gone completely unnoticed if it weren't for one defining trait that made him stick out over the rest in his incoming class—his thirst for how to improve simple tasks. He had no extraordinary characteristics physically. He didn't possess extraordinary movement skill or strength. He was a normal guy who would have blended into the crowd if he had let himself. He did, however, have an incredible knack for working extremely hard at basic, ordinary things. He was the kind of player who asked lots of questions and wanted to know how to do the basic things correctly. When he received instruction and coaching on movement skill, lifting technique, nutrition, etc., he executed his style of relentless attack on ordinary movements and knowledge. As a young college player, even before his first camp practice at Boston College, he displayed the drive to address ordinary tasks as game-changing opportunities. He would train and practice as if every situation was the same—the chance to win. His attention to detail in all aspects was unmatched in how he went about his everyday routine.

Over the three years I had the privilege to coach Luke, it was obvious his development came from that basic drive. He put on the necessary weight, gained the necessary strength, and improved on the necessary movement skill because he didn't wait for the perfect moment; he made each moment the perfect time to improve. And it started with him executing ordinary movements, training techniques, and preparation to perfection. He approached warm-ups the same as third downs. He attacked basic lifting technique trying to perfect the movement that everyone else saw as "I got this." He executed drill after drill and focused on the detail of each basic movement. If it wasn't right, he did it again and again until it was right— then executed it over and over with the same competitive approach as if he had failed the time before. He constantly watched film and broke down not only his opponents' but also his own tendencies and weaknesses. He took the time to focus on the ordinary details of success.

There is no one particular standout moment I can point to to define Luke's display of game-changing ability; rather I can point to his entire career as a football player at both Boston College and in the NFL. At Boston College his ability to focus on routine ordinary tasks helped him achieve the following awards in just three years of playing:

- Three-time first team All-American (2009, 2010, 2011)
- Three-time first team All–Atlantic Coast Conference (ACC) (2009, 2010, 2011)
- ACC Athlete of the Year (2012)
- ACC Defensive Rookie of the Year (2009)
- Two-time Bowl Defensive Most Valuable Player (2009, 2011)
- Butkus Award Winner (2011)
- Lombardi Award Winner (2011)
- Lott IMPACT Trophy Winner (2011)
- Bronko Nagurski Trophy Winner (2011)
- Jack Lambert Award Winner (2011)
- FWAA 75th Anniversary All-American Team (2015)

His NFL achievements include:

- NFL Rookie of the Year (2012)
- NFL Defensive Player of the Year (2013)

These two gentlemen are only a small snapshot of the many I have coached, and am coaching to this day, who show this ability. Most of the athletes I have coached never made it to the professional levels of sports, but many have excelled in their chosen fields. All of those individuals have excelled because they all had that one, small, almost undiscernible trait—the uncanny ability to concentrate on doing the ordinary better than the next person. They realized that games are won and lost, careers are made or broken, and leaders are made and strengthened by handling business when no one is watching. When the "game" seems boring to most, they are still engaged and thirsting for improvement. They don't concentrate on extraordinary effort or ability. They simply take ordinary tasks and master them. They make the ordinary a competitive advantage over their competition.

They take what many people see as boring, mundane, "it will take care of itself because I've done it a million times" tasks and put all their focus, energy, and attention into perfecting them even more. They never rise to the occasion in pressure situations; they simply just rely on their ability to execute simple, everyday technique and leadership skills to perfection. No matter what the profession, when the pressure mounts, people tune in to watch for either exhilarating victory or exceptional failure. When an individual rises above the rest, it is more about others falling than them rising (Jason Loscalzo, pers. comm.).

> **"The master said, 'Well done, my good and faithful servant. You have been faithful in handling this small amount, so now I will give you many more responsibilities. Let's celebrate together!'"—Matthew 25:23 (Bible Gateway 2017)**

In summary, the playmaker is often one shift in attitude, discipline, or mindset away from moving into a position where the status of game changer would dominate his or her personal and professional life. While playmakers want to *get* more, they often skip the vital trait of first *becoming* more. American businessman and business philosopher Jim Rohn pointed out the error in that thinking by suggesting that in order to get "more than you've got," you must first "become more than you are" (Jim Rohn (a), AZ Quotes 2017).

That being said, where in your thinking, habits, or daily routine must you *become* more in order to move into unstoppable game changer status? Since no one will—or can—do it for you, what will you do about it, beginning right now?

When discussing what he prioritized when recruiting, Coach Crean put it this way:

> You have to look at their upside; do they have a high ceiling? You can't get hung up or overly excited about

where they're at, but where they can go. Someone who really wants to compete at whatever they want to do, you can feel it. Yogi Ferrell always had that. Some guys can fake it, and eventually their lack of awareness, lack of being driven, and the need to always be pushed by someone else come out. People say, "Does he have a nose for the ball?" But it's really more like "Will he get his nose in the mix?" Some guys won't. They hate contact. Yogi never shied away from contact (Tom Crean, pers. comm.).

How about you? Based on your attitude, character, desire, and willingness to develop necessary disciplines, how high is your ceiling? Will you shy away from the contact of change, risk, sacrifice, and discomfort necessary to move your thinking and performance from playmaker to game changer status? Will you shy away from contact, or will you seek it out?

Mission Unstoppable

To become an unstoppable game changer, consider and act on the following four key differences between the valuable playmaker and the essential game changer that were discussed in this chapter:

1. Being less consistent versus fanatically consistent.
2. Relying on external versus intrinsic motivation.
3. Having a mindset of pride and selfishness versus humility and team focus.
4. Seeking the extraordinary versus committing to do the ordinary both extraordinarily and consistently well.

As you evaluate your own mindset and performance, which of the tendencies dominates your daily thinking and actions more? What adjustments in thinking and performance will you make to spend more time in game changer status?

Use additional and helpful resources to help yourself and others create game changer performance. Subscribe to "Tuesdays with Sam

Chand," in which free and brief mentoring videos are sent to your e-mail each Tuesday to help accelerate your growth.

Game changers do not wait for the things around them to change; they first change what's within them, so they can change what's around them.

CHAPTER 4

The Game Changer

Being in a league of your own as a game changer does not mean that you are number one in a league that everyone else is in. Instead, it is about being so good at what you do that you create another league, and you are the only one in it.

If you have been paying attention as you read the past three chapters, you already know quite a bit about game changers, and are aware of some mental adjustments you may need to make to work and live in more of a game changer status. Here is a quick review of key points, as well as additional insights to solidify your understanding of nine things it takes to become unstoppable.

1. **Game changers are not born; they are made.** But they are made from the inside out; they cannot be forced, or persuaded from the outside in. You can listen to pep talks, attend lectures on the value of hard work and paying the price, and study countless examples—as I am providing in this book—of the traits others developed and applied to reach game changer status. But until you decide to think differently, stop blaming or making excuses, change your behaviors, replace unproductive habits with healthy

habits, and get so focused on your dreams—and why you want them—that you become unstoppable, you are resigned to spend more of your time bouncing around the undertaker, caretaker, and playmaker performance categories, while game changer status eludes you.

There is no question that your thinking can be influenced from the outside in, or that you can influence another's thinking from the outside in (just as I am endeavoring to do with this book, with my game changer seminars, my *The Game Changer Life* podcast, and more), but *you* have to decide to act on the challenge or on the information, inspiration, or motivation offered. Most will listen and agree that working and living to the fullest, to their greatest potential, makes sense. As a result of outside stimulation, some will make changes but soon revert back to their old thinking and behaviors. But a few—a small handful—will flip a switch in their minds, begin the journey to game changer status, and never look back.

Attitude, not conditions, governs contentment and greatly determines destiny.

I can recall an essential piece of outside stimulation that helped flip my own switch. I was 90 days into a new job selling cars at Parnell Chrysler/Plymouth/Jeep more than three decades ago, and my results were in the middle of the pack, far from the top of the sales board. The dealer, Harold Parnell, had a habit of writing messages on the bottoms of paycheck statements. Some were positive; others were downright ornery. One payday he had written the first and only note he ever inscribed on my pay statement: "We're waiting for you to make your move. Show us you're number one."

Up to that point I was not even thinking in terms of being the best at that dealership. I was still learning the ropes, trying to fit in, and determining if car sales was the best way to provide for my young family. But that day, a switch went off in my mind.

Mr. Parnell saw something in me I had not yet discovered about myself. He provoked a rise in sights, a new thinking, and a higher aspiration. I went on to become the top salesperson at Parnell Chrysler for 15 straight months following his message, after which I was offered a management job elsewhere. To make a long story short, six years after starting fresh on the floor as a salesperson in my first-ever auto-sales job, I was the number-two man in a $300 million dealership group, the equivalent of which would be substantially larger in today's dollars. To Harold Parnell's credit, he paid enough attention to see something in me and challenge me, and to my credit I decided to change my thinking and my behaviors because of his affirmation.

Another can plant a seed in your life, but you own the choice to either water it or let it die of neglect.

When Phil Beckner coached future National Basketball Association (NBA) all-star Damian Lillard at Weber State, Lillard was MVP of his conference during his sophomore year, and everyone started to realize how special he could be. And a challenge from Beckner helped lift him to the next level. Despite Lillard's personal achievement that year, his team failed to make the National Collegiate Athletic Association (NCAA) tournament, and that set off a fire within him. Beckner decided to stoke the flames with a positive provocation by saying, "You can't just work hard Monday through Friday and let up on the weekend. You can't just be a 50/50 guy where one day you put in extra work, and then the next day you do what's required."

Lillard hit back, saying, "I'm not a 50/50 guy."

Beckner replied, "Yes, you are. On weekends, you go to football games and other events rather than working out; you do it five days out of seven."

Lillard replied, "I'll put in extra work every single day!" (Phil Beckner, pers. comm.).

And he started to do just that: before and after practice, during spring break, and on weekends starting at 8:00 AM shooting with Beckner on Saturdays (which pretty much eliminated any late Friday nights). Then Lillard took the next step and asked Beckner to work out with him on Sundays, and the coach told him, "I'm not doing it on Sunday with you. You have to do it on your own. Show me you can do it without someone pushing you. I'll open the gym for you, and then you're on your own."

One Sunday after Coach Beckner opened the gym and left Lillard to work out, he texted later, "How many did you make?" The reply he received was "Made 250 shots."

The next Sunday, Beckner did the same thing and got Lillard's texted reply, "Made 300." The third consecutive Sunday, Beckner opened the gym. This time, however, he stayed and hid to see if Lillard was really shooting, and watched him sink 400 shots. Then he got the text from Lillard: "400 shots."

On the fourth week, Beckner, completely trusting Lillard now, opened the gym and left. After his customary, "How many?" text, Lillard replied, "675. My shoulder hurts." Not 675 *shots*, mind you—675 *made* shots.

Damian Lillard had put in extra work for 37 straight days when Beckner told him, "Take a day off. You're not a 50/50 guy anymore" (Phil Beckner, pers. comm.).

Don't lead a horse to water and try to talk it into drinking. Find out what makes the horse thirsty. Which brings up a key point: What makes *you* thirsty? You have to know yourself to move yourself.

2. **Game changers do the ordinary extraordinarily well, and consistently well.** As a result, they appear to do the exceptional, when they are actually just reaping the entirely predictable harvest from the consistent seeds of discipline, attention to detail, continual improvement, and extra work they have sown over time.

One of my mentors, the late and great Jim Rohn, had keen insight into this point. Here are some notes from Rohn's *The Weekend Seminar* in 1999 that are just as relevant today as they were then: "Failure is nothing more than an accumulation of wrong decisions repeated over again, every day. Failure isn't an accident. Success is nothing more than an accumulation of right decisions repeated over again, every day. Success isn't an accident. If you don't like what you're reaping, sow something else!" (Rohn 1999).

"To create something exceptional, your mindset must be focused relentlessly on the smallest detail."
—Giorgio Armani (AZ Quotes 2017)

3. **Game changers are good cultural fits.** In some cases they may not even have the same levels of skill, knowledge, talent, or experience as some undertakers, caretakers, or playmakers. But it is the incessantly constant manner with which they apply what they *do* have, and add value to the culture, that sets them apart. And that relentless approach is rooted in the right mindset.

Scott Cross is the head basketball coach for the Mavericks at the University of Texas at Arlington, a team on the rise and gaining national recognition for its success. Notice what characteristics stand out to Coach Cross as defining who game changers are, what they are not, and also what they do:

> At UT Arlington, we have had three record-breaking seasons since 2011–2012. In '11–'12, we won the Southland Conference, won 24 games, and had a 16-game win streak. Unfortunately, we lost in the semifinals of the conference tournament, and because of this we had to settle on the NIT [National Invitational Tournament] instead of the NCAA Tournament. Last year (2015–2016), we also won 24 games and were 13–3 before our leading scorer and rebounder, Kevin Hervey,

had to undergo ACL [anterior cruciate ligament] surgery. We were very fortunate to have nonconference road wins last season over Ohio State, Memphis, UTEP [University of Texas at El Paso], North Texas, and Rice. In 2016–2017, we finished the season at 27–9, and were ranked #11 in *College Insider*'s Mid-Major Top 25.

When considering "game changers," I think about the guy or guys who helped us overachieve. Lamarcus "Jug" Reed was definitely one of our most talented players in '11–'12. However, over the past two seasons, the three players who I would call our game changers are not our most talented players. I would call Jalen Jones, Jorge Bilbao, and Drew Charles our game changers. I think the reason that they are game changers is because all of these guys have embraced our culture and values. We can summarize our culture and values with this statement: "We are a tough, competitive, selfless basketball team that communicates and takes ownership in everything that we do." I guarantee that all of my game changers have been extremely coachable players.

I never had to worry about the little things when Jug was the leader of our basketball team. If we had a team function at 9 AM, he would have the entire team dressed appropriately 15 minutes ahead of schedule. Nobody was ever late for a bus or team outing. I did not realize that he was doing all of this until he was gone. When he left, our culture suffered for a couple of years as I realized that we needed to recruit more guys like Jug. I had just finished reading an article about Coach Chris Petersen when he was at Boise State, and he talked about recruiting "OKGs" (Our Kind of Guys). OKGs for Coach Petersen were high-production, low-ego players. My definition of an OKG was someone who was tough and competitive. I made it a point to recruit more guys just like Jug. The signing of Jalen Jones was a direct result of us wanting to sign OKGs.

Over the last year, I have expanded my definition of OKGs to be guys who embody our core values: *tough, competitive, selfless* basketball players who *communicate* and take *ownership* in everything that they do. I actually turned down a Top 100 basketball player because I did not feel that he would fit into our culture here. I want guys who are "culture" guys. I believe that a championship basketball team can have one or two players who do not embody all of the attributes of our culture, but the other 13 had better be pretty darn close.

I can remember that we told Lamarcus "Jug" Reed after his sophomore season that he needed to become a better three-point shooter and that he needed to shoot 10,000 shots a month. We started a monthly "10K" shooting club. Lamarcus embraced this and shot 10,000 shots almost every single month. And, over the last two years of his career, he was one of the best shooters in the Southland Conference. Here were his year-by-year three-point shooting percentages:

- 2008–2009: 4–14 (28.6%)
- 2009–2010: 12–45 (26.7%)
- 2010–2011: 46–119 (38.7%)
- 2011–2012: 64–166 (38.6%)

Jug embraced the process and culture of getting better every single day and helped establish this for future UT Arlington basketball teams (Scott Cross, pers. comm.).

Talent without character is unsustainable. Character without talent brings frustration. Character combined with talent becomes unstoppable.

4. **Game changers are more intrinsically motivated, and thus committed to self-improvement.** In fact, they are obsessed with it. Their primary objective is to become better than their

former best. As a result, they often become *the* best at what they do. Their mantra is: "Yesterday ended last night. I will prove myself over again today."

Dr. Jim Afremow, author of two outstanding books on performance, *The Champion's Mind* and *The Champion's Comeback,* observes:

> Along with talent, there are several characteristics that help push a person to excellence. These include discipline and forming the habit of hard work. There is mental toughness and handling pressure, both on the field and off, and both of which are better handled if one has a higher cause or purpose. There is an attitude of gratitude rather than a sense of entitlement. There is the most important characteristic, belief in oneself. And day-to-day, throughout life, there is a continual desire to get better. This is a growth mindset that is ingrained young and really never tapers off. With these themes in mind, the best ask themselves this question: "What do I do today, knowing that it helps me be better tomorrow?" (Dr. Jim Afremow, pers. comm.).

Sony/ATV Music's Troy Tomlinson adds, "They are competitive, but like a golfer, thinking: 'Sure, there are a lot of folks on the field, but I'm really competing with myself'" (Troy Tomlinson, pers. comm.).

To paraphrase Jim Rohn: Game changers know that their game, business, and life get better once they do. They never wish it were easier; they wish they were better—Jim Rohn (b), (AZ Quotes 2017)

5. **The game changer errs on the side of being personally humble rather than showy, and has a voracious ambition for the team to do well.** He or she believes that by continuing to

grow and excel, and being a clutch member of the team, he or she can inspire and lift others to a higher level of intensity, desire, and performance.

Family First Life's Shawn Meaike explains how he learned to be a clutch teammate from his time playing baseball: "I had a baseball coach while I was growing up named John Ellis who was a Major League Baseball player for many years. He coached me for only a few months in the summer of 1991, but he taught me about being a game changer. During a Legion baseball game one summer, he pulled me aside before I went up to bat in a tie game in the bottom of the ninth. He said, 'Leaders get it done every time the game is on the line; that is what makes them leaders. Anybody can get a hit up 10–0, or down 10–0'" (Shawn Meaike, pers. comm.).

Game changers understand that on any given day, at least one teammate will not be totally dialed in mentally and/or physically. They also know that they will never be that person.

6. **Game changers renounce excuses as the DNA of under-achievers, and focus on the aspects of their lives and jobs they can control.**

    Karate world champion Johnny Gyro explains well the immense rewards for those who renounce the options and ease of making excuses and quitting, and decide to pay the price necessary to reach their dreams:

    I had a never-give-up, quitting-is-not-an-option outlook. I employed that unforgiving method in my training as well. If you want to fight hard, you must train hard. It's just that simple. Having talent is one thing, and I felt I had the talent to make a very good fighter, but I wanted to become an outstanding fighter with a name that stood for excellence. If I wanted to gain the respect of all the other veteran fighters, no one would respect excuses. I fought every fight like it was the "big one"—the one that mattered the most—because along the way, each fight would bring me that much closer to my goal. One loss while the other competitors in my division won would set me back, and in my mind that was an entirely unacceptable option. Achieving a goal like mine required me to outsmart, outthink, and outperform everyone else. That meant fighting like it was my last match every single time.

Before long, at almost every tournament I went to, I saw more and more well-trained, disciplined fighters pack up and leave before fighting in my division. This told me I was doing something very right because the momentum I felt was palpable—momentum, not through intimidation, but through actual accomplishment. Intimidation is an empty vice that is based on ego. Among the veteran karate fighters, I had many great friends and many that I respected as formidable opponents. However, while in the ring during competition, the only thing that mattered was fighting to win. I wanted to be judged and remembered for my talent, for my abilities, and for my never-give-up and take-no-prisoners performance every single time. After all, being a fighter requires you to count only on yourself—you do it alone, and I preferred it that way. I didn't have anyone holding me back, telling me how I should keep my goals realistic or changing my direction. I achieved my goal, my success, through my direction, my dedication, and with unfaltering determination. Even with undeniable talent and potential, without direction, without dedication and the determination to see it through without exception, success will always elude the fool who tries to rely on talent alone. There are infinitely talented individuals in this world of all ages, diversities, and variations, and we will never know who they are, what they look like, or what their names are if they lack the desire, direction, and determination to propel them to victory.

My name, my achievements, and my records speak for themselves—and they also speak for me. Make no mistake—the road was never smooth or easy, and it rarely is for any goal worth achieving. I suffered many injuries and broken bones along the way (a broken jaw, a broken eye socket, a broken nose, a broken eardrum, a fractured skull, a torn ACL, and countless concussions). Likewise, I am not proud of injuring other karate fighters during matches when I did, but it was part of the game, especially back then when protective gear wasn't required or worn. Many have asked, "Why do it?" and my response is because becoming the number 1-rated fighter in our great nation mattered to me. It was everything. It was more important for me to find out if I could achieve what I set out to do, as challenging as it was; or, was I the type to just talk about wanting it? Taking on that challenge defined me. I became less about talking about my goals and much more about being programmed to do whatever it takes. That was and still is my personal mindset, which is much more than a philosophy. That mental process of winning remains with me to this day and is responsible for my life's journey and successes that followed. When I opened my karate studio 22 years ago this year, my drive for success in business was ignited and propelled by the same winning mental toughness and tenacious spirit that I had then and still have as a fighter. Identify your desire, devise your direction, and sustain your determination to ward off making excuses for yourself. Hold yourself accountable so that above all else you can respect yourself (Johnny Gyro, pers. comm.).

Did you catch that last sentence? "Hold yourself accountable so that above all else you can respect yourself." "Respect Yourself" is the slogan on the back of the Johnny Gyro karate shirts we work out in at Master Gyro's studio. But respect must be earned, and a ton of folks in our snowflake culture today have regressed from being hungry and "huddled masses yearning to be free" to "coddled masses yearning for what's free." They say things like, "I'd love to do what you do" or "My dream is to have what you have." The question is: Are they willing to do what *you did* to do what you do, and to have what you have? In most cases, not a chance. They have lost sight of the fact that earning it, busting your rear end for it, and making sacrifices for getting what you want *just flat out feels great!*

Millions today have shelves or drawers littered with worthless, twelfth-place participant ribbons they were granted for showing up, but not for stepping up. In the game changer's world, there are no participant ribbons and no participant paychecks. You earn it, you deserve it, or you go without it; and you stop making excuses for why you don't do it, and stop whining if you didn't get it. "Hold yourself accountable so that above all else you can respect yourself" is a game changer mantra. It also means that failing to give your best, and to own it, creates the conditions under which you think less of yourself. And others will, too. Whether in the workplace or on the field of play, you should expect that people would grant you common courtesies as a fellow human being; but if you want respect, then live and perform in a way that is worthy of it. In case you missed it the first time: earn it, deserve it, or go without it.

> Game changers may lose, but they do not quit. A loser comes up short, learns something, and comes back again more determined. A quitter simply gives up because it hurts or because it was hard, and then blames someone or something else.

7. **Game changers change and risk before they have to; thus, they do so from a position of strength and do not wait until their vision is impaired by desperation.**

Troy Tomlinson comments, "They have an ability to be in a constant state of evolution as an artist, and to embrace revolution as an artist" (Troy Tomlinson, pers. comm.).

Sadly, prosperity drains urgency. The more successful people are or become, the more comfortable they become with what and who they are. Eventually, they are outgrown and lose their relevance.

> "There are risks and costs to action. But they are far less than the long-range risks of comfortable inaction."
> —John F. Kennedy (AZ Quotes 2017)

8. **Game changers want to be coached.**

They do not consider constructive criticism, instruction, correction, setbacks, or losses as failure, but as helpful feedback. They adjust their behaviors and grow because of it.

Athletic Director Kevin Ozee observes, "While most get offended, game changers accept constructive criticism as a compliment. There is no losing for a game changer because he or she is always learning, even when faced with a setback" (Kevin Ozee, pers. comm.).

To sum it up, Ken Blanchard said it well: "Feedback is the breakfast of champions" (AZ Quotes 2017).

> Undertakers are uncoachable, caretakers do not want coaching, playmakers want to be coached sometimes, and game changers want to be coached always.

9. **A game changer answers the question "How much is enough?" with "All that I possibly can."** He or she believes that being able to do more but choosing not to is just a sanitized sort of embezzlement.

This is illustrated in LAPD Captain Palka's description of the relentless work ethic of one of his game changers, Lieutenant Hamed "Mo" Mohammadi:

Mo used to say, "If someone works 60 hours a week, I'll work 70. If they work 70, I'll work 80." His relentlessness and his thirst for learning are incredible. He was always a bulldog and would take on any task that I or one of my bosses needed done well.

He is rooted in policy and is smart. He is a military buff and is fascinated by military leadership. He is willing to sacrifice everything to make the *team* better—to get the job done. His youth and lack of experience can rub the wrong way with many who are simply intimidated by his demand of self. He is ruthless at times, but in a paramilitary organization he is needed desperately because he will burn the midnight oil to get the job done. He is a game changer, as he is one you can always turn to who will say, "Yes, sir. Let's go get it done." He also brings energy, enthusiasm, and humor to the culture (Cory Palka, pers. comm.).

"All I can" goes beyond a quantity of work. In a game changer's world it also applies to doing all that is possible to turn out the best work possible. In other words, "good enough is never good enough." If you watch prime-time television, you have probably seen the work of Andrew Dettmann, an American television writer and producer working in one-hour network drama. Working consistently for more than 20 years, he is credited as writer and/or producer on more than 350 hours of television. His credits include CSI, *Chicago Med, Body of Proof,* and *Numb3rs,* to name just a few. What Dettmann says about his own "good enough is never good enough" philosophy applies to anyone aspiring to excellence in any endeavor:

In series television, the fundamental responsibility of a writer/producer is generating scripts. Without scripts, the whole production mechanism grinds to a halt, which is a disastrous and very expensive circumstance to be in—cast and crew sitting around on the set with nothing to film. Nobody at the studio or network is going to be happy. *Quality scripts. On time.* That's the job.

But it's a tricky business because, ultimately, writing is subjective. You're creating a product, the script, which has no concrete or definitive measure of good or bad, right or wrong. As a result, you very often reach a point in the process where you have a script that's "good enough." You could bundle it up, send it off to the set, and the end result would be a perfectly acceptable episode of television. And there's usually great temptation to go that route—get this one done, move on to the next. But that sort of thinking is a trap, one you want to avoid.

Never think it's okay to slide by on "good enough." There's always a way to improve the script—reimagining, reworking, rewriting, even when you don't have to. Until the episode has been filmed and the cameras turned off, the opportunity still exists to improve what you have. So don't squander that opportunity. Keep working on the product. Find another way to make it better. Even when you think the improvements might be too small or subtle to be noticed, make them anyway. People will notice. Obviously, it's a philosophy that goes beyond the narrow world of television writing, which is why I think it's worthy of mentioning (Andrew Dettmann, pers. comm.).

Dettmann adds more value to developing a game changer mindset as he discusses the importance of flexibility—a concept absolutely appalling to caretakers—by saying:

A second philosophy that I've found indispensable is this: always be *flexible*. That's something you learn to embrace not because you want to, but because you have to. In television production (like anywhere, I suppose), things can change quickly and without notice. Filming locations fall through at the last moment. Weather can disrupt plans to film outdoors. Actors get sick, or maybe just refuse to say the scripted lines. You have to be adaptable. You have to be flexible enough to make changes to the script, right now, on the fly, without sacrificing quality or disturbing the continuity of the storyline. That may sound simple, but it's not. As writers, we tend to get entrenched in the script as written. We're resistant to changes that aren't story driven. But in situations like the above, you don't have a choice; and the more flexible you are going in, the better off you're going to be when the moment inevitably comes.

Certainly, there are countless factors and variables that contribute to the longevity of any career, and I'm not implying any simple, two-pronged path to success. But in my own experience, I make an effort to keep two things in the front of my mind: "Good enough" is never good enough. And "stay flexible" (Andrew Dettmann, pers. comm.).

> **Work ethic is more than the hours you put in; it is what you put into the hours. What good does it do to put in more hours, if you have not been putting the right things into those hours?**

In summary, you should be encouraged by this chapter because you now (it is hoped) embrace the fact that whether you become a game changer depends on you, and you alone. No one can, or should, make that decision for you. *You* get to choose to become unstoppable—to work harder; to give up excuses; to focus more on what you can control; to be more humble, hungry, persistent, and focused; and to grow. So the good news is that no one can stop you. The not-so-good news is that if you fall short of developing the mindset and habits that make you unstoppable, *you* are to blame. You own it either way. And that is exactly how a game changer would want it to be.

Climbing higher requires making trade-offs. Decide which compromises, activities, habits, attitudes, and associations you must give up in order to go up.

Mission Unstoppable

To become an unstoppable game changer, consider and act on the following (we tackled some of these factors in Chapter 3; so, for now, let's focus on point number 6, from earlier in this chapter):

1. Considering that game changers renounce excuses and focus on the aspects of their jobs and lives they can control, which excuses have you tended to lean on to rationalize not being more successful than you are?

   - An ineffective leader that you are suffering under.
   - Those you work with.
   - Something a competitor is doing that you cannot match.
   - A unique aspect of the area you are in.
   - Lack of training.
   - Someone else not doing enough to motivate you.
   - The economy, the time of the year, where you were born, your parents, the fact you have never been in touch with your "inner something or another," and the like.

2. Consider the wasted power, energy, and time you are giving to one or more of these excuses, and how in return you are only becoming more frustrated, more powerless, and more pathetic. Then, identify aspects of your job and life you actually *can* control, and choose to invest more focus into those areas. Here are a few to help shift your gaze from outside the window toward what is in the mirror:

   - Will you choose the right attitude, work ethic, level of discipline, and character?
   - Will you spend more time with people who elevate you and challenge you?

- Will you seek out, insist on, and act because of feedback?
- Will you spend time both at work and away from work investing more in the things that matter most, or doing what is easy and amusing?
- Will you plan your day or wing it?
- Will you put in the extra work or practice with baseline effort?
- Will you follow the process or take shortcuts?
- Will you ask for help or remain prideful?
- Will you put yourself on a personal growth program, or continue to wait for life to come along and improve you?
- Will you spend more time reading, studying, and perfecting your craft and less time watching reality television, reading garbage media, playing video games, and competing in fantasy football leagues?
- Will you speak in terms of solutions, or just whine about problems?
- Will you speak to people about issues, or gossip about people?
- Will you choose to overlook trivial nonsense that doesn't really matter, or decide to take offense and waste time and energy pouting, debating, and putting people in their place?

3. Use additional and helpful resources to help yourself and others create game changer performance. Take the "Become a Game Changer Power Program" video course in the Online Power Programs for Individuals section at www.AndersonVT.com. It is a four-chapter program, totaling two hours.

At the end of the day, game changers realize they are not victims of circumstances. They are products of their choices, and they redouble their efforts to make more right choices daily. And every day means every day—EDMED!

CHAPTER 5

It's About Decisions, Not Conditions

The Law of the Mirror: It is my daily decisions, not external conditions, that determine how far I go and how fast I get there. Thus, upgrading my life to game changer status is based on my decisions and is not contingent on conditions I cannot control.

After reading the nine insights that were provided in Chapter 4—regarding elevating your mindset, performance, and life to game changer status—one thing should be abundantly clear: working and living in a manner where game changer status (being consistently energized, focused, and unstoppable) dominates your existence is a matter of decisions, not conditions. And for that you should be grateful, because this puts *you* in charge of *your* destiny. After all, decisions are within your control, whereas conditions are not. So the good news is you get to choose whether you will become a game changer. The bad news is that, if you don't make the leap to a point where game changer status dominates both your work and your life, then it is all on you; you cannot blame others or stuff. You have to fault your thinking, choices, and behaviors.

Frankly, an aspiring game changer would not want it any other way. Game changers in the making are not waiting for some universal, cosmic welfare system to lift them out of obscurity, subsidize their performance, and give them a handout or a hand up to get started. Rather, their philosophy is to count on the things they can control: mindset, faith, persistence, hunger, and growth to propel them to their dreams.

Granted, in the politically correct times we live in, unpopular truths (as presented in this book) are becoming scarcer. Because no one wants to offend you, they instead let you just get by, blame, make excuses, believe you are a victim, and think you are something special when you are one of many. Most dangerously, because we are reluctant to make someone feel bad or to appear judgmental, we have stopped talking about consequences for one's actions or for what is illegal, slothful, or sinful, and have come close to purging absolutes from our culture and conversations altogether. "Everyone's a winner" and "Anything is permissible as long as it makes you feel good" are the popular palaver of politically correct morons who fail to grasp that one's character and culture are greatly determined by what you do not accept or tolerate—that in the real-world trenches of performance there are losers, that there is wrong, and that participation trophies are pathetic and farcical mockeries of performance that blow the smoke of false self-esteem up the backside of the undeserving.

Frankly, political correctness in speech, in behaviors, and within cultures will stunt your growth because it is dishonest. It takes the truth and trivializes it, sanitizes it, compromises it, and marginalizes it so you never truly face what the real issue is. And if you do not face it you cannot fix it. Political correctness takes what is bad or wrong and makes it right, and takes what is right or good and makes it wrong. In a sense, political correctness would have you believe it is entirely possible to pick up a turd by the clean end. The media—which I spend *very* little time with—will not even use words like *undeserving*, *sin*, or *illegal* anymore because they sound judgmental and harsh.

Thus, we have stopped talking about tried-and-true principles of human behavior: that there *is* cause and effect, and sowing and reaping. Let me put this in perspective: If people break into my house, they are there illegally. They are not an "undocumented" houseguest, and I am not giving them a welfare allowance, sending their kids to college, or paying their medical bills. There will be painful consequences for their trespass, and that is what aspiring game changers must come to understand. Wrong choices have consequences, and, when you choose a behavior, you choose the consequences that come with it; you are not a victim. However, when you choose the right behaviors, you are also choosing the pleasant consequences that eventually come with them. You did not just "get lucky." Either way, what could be fairer than that?

Your Personal Philosophy

An important mentor in my life was author, speaker, and businessman Jim Rohn. Mr. Rohn taught that if you want to change your life, you must change your philosophy, and that everyone has a philosophy, the primary questions being: "Where has yours brought you today?" and "Where is it taking you in the future?" Are there some flaws in your philosophy that have held you back that must be upgraded, tweaked, or completely deleted? Anyone wanting to live more of his or her life in game changer status will have changes to make in his or her philosophy concerning factors such as taking responsibility, continually improving, focusing on controllables, serving others, and intentionally building a resilient mindset. Like game changers, the undertakers, caretakers, and playmakers similarly all have philosophies that dominate their thinking, and thus their lives. The results that people from these groups reap are a direct result of that philosophy. For them to change their results, they must first change their behaviors. And in order for that to happen, they must change their thinking and upgrade their personal philosophies.

What follows are five additional insights into the mindsets of those who can be declared unstoppable game changers and how they became that way.

1. **Game changers are far from perfect, and they do not always have outstanding days, weeks, or months.** But, because of their hunger, resilience, and ability to focus, they do not get off track as often or stay off track as long as other performers do. They continually strive for excellence, as LAPD Captain Cory Palka succinctly explains about one of his game changers, Hollywood Lieutenant Mario Mota: "He works tirelessly and does it quietly with his zest and zeal to be *always* excellent" (Cory Palka, pers. comm.).

We all get off track. But to live at game changer status you will need to do so less often; and, when you get off track, shorten the duration.

2. **Game changers think differently and have developed a robust "I own it" philosophy toward work and life.** Thus, the power to become a game changer performer at whatever you do is within your own grasp. *You* get to choose. Your thinking will most likely need to be transformed—not merely tweaked—to consistently perform at a game changer level. That will not happen overnight, but it can happen over time. To transform your thinking, you may need to change your associations and your habits, as well as what you read, study, or listen to. You will also need to stop blaming whatever you have been blaming and give up your go-to excuses. But that will be the best trade-off you will ever make! Coach Phil Beckner offers additional razor-sharp perspective through highlights of the clear differences between the prevailing mindset philosophies of playmakers and game changers:

- **Source of motivation.** The playmaker is externally motivated. The game changer is internally motivated.
- **Relationship to time.** The playmaker is on time and ready for direction. The game changer is early and prepared.
- **When preparing a daily schedule.** The playmaker is curious about what will happen. The game changer is disciplined to a set routine.

- **Cultural buy-in.** A playmaker is the person who is being *pulled* along. The game changer *pushes* others along.
- **Talk versus actions.** The playmaker prefers words and comforting lies. The game changer prefers behaviors and true criticism.
- **Handling weaknesses.** The playmaker gives excuses and neglects accountability. The game changer looks within and takes ownership.
- **The difference in thoughts, phrases, and words.**
  Playmaker: "Look what you did to me." Game changer: "Look what I did to myself."
  Playmaker: "I can't succeed because everyone is against me." Game changer: "I will succeed if the world is against me."
  Playmaker: "I think I'm getting attacked." Game changer: "I'm getting pushed."
  Playmaker: "I wish people would leave me alone." Game changer: "I wish I had more people to make me better."
  Playmaker: "I accept human nature." Game changer: "It's my job to fight human nature" (Phil Beckner, pers. comm.).

Game changers think what others are not willing to think, do what the masses are not willing to do, go where the herd does not want to go, and give up soft habits that the mediocre find comfort in—all so that they can one day have a life that those who are unwilling to sacrifice for can only dream about. Coach Scott Cross at the University of Texas at Arlington infused a "#TakeTheStairs" philosophy into his team that the average masses would find bothersome and extreme—which reminds us again why it is not crowded at the top and why there is intense competition among the average, ordinary, and not outstanding. It also helps explain the immense success of his program:

> One of our mantras at UT Arlington has been to Take the Stairs. Unfortunately, Rory Vaden beat me to it and wrote a very good book by the same name: *Take the Stairs*. I was excited to read *Take the Stairs* and loved the entire book; but I also felt that this was exactly what I have been

preaching to my team over the last year. #TakeTheStairs started for me during the 2014–2015 season after returning from a long road trip to nothing but ice and snow. I decided to jog around our basketball arena late that evening since it was cold and icy outside. As I was rounding the corner, I noticed that the elevator opened up right as I was passing by. Inside were a couple of my players, and I kind of gave them a head nod that signaled, "What's up?" But then, after a couple of steps, I realized what had happened. My players (I wasn't sure how many were in the elevator at the time) decided to take an elevator up from the hallway by the locker room, instead of walking out to the arena and up the stairs—which would have been quicker since the arena elevators are very slow. As I continued to run, I started stewing.

It has always been a pet peeve of mine when my players use a hotel elevator to go up and down one or two floors instead of taking the stairs. I always take the stairs for several reasons: (1) It is quicker if it is less than three floors; (2) I cannot stand waiting in one place when I could be moving; (3) I want my players to know that I don't just talk the talk, but I walk the walk; and (4) I want my players to be tough in everything that they do and to be conscious of every decision that they make, including taking the elevator or stairs.

I couldn't sleep that night because of the laziness of my team. We had a game the very next day. We watched film at 9 AM, and then we shot at 10 AM. Before we started shoot around, I asked my players, "Who were the people in the elevator that I saw as I was jogging around the arena?" Five of them raised their hands. I explained to them that those elevators are for people who cannot walk, that they were blessed with two legs and feet that work, and that they were taking their ability to walk for granted. I asked them how a veteran who had his legs blown off in war would think about them taking that elevator when they have the ability to use their own two legs. If they feel that sorry for themselves because we had a long practice and they were tired, then we have no chance of succeeding as a basketball team. In addition, if they did not change their mentality and toughen up, then they have no chance for success later in life. I then had each person who took the elevator partner up with a player who had not and "wheelbarrow" from midcourt up the stairs and back down on their hands, while their partners carried their legs. It took about five minutes, and their arms were pretty tired, but I think the point sank in very well for the entire team.

We went on to win the game that night and had one of our best performances of the entire season. Almost two years has passed since that day; but #TakeTheStairs has been my motto and mantra, and I have been preaching it over and over to my team. All of my "game changers" are #TakeTheStairs guys (Scott Cross, pers. comm.).

To paraphrase the great Jim Rohn's *The Weekend Seminar*: Philosophy drives attitude, attitude drives actions, actions drive results, and results drive lifestyles. Thus, if you don't like your lifestyle, then you need to look at your results. If you don't like your results, look at your actions. If you don't like your actions, take a look at your attitude. And, if you don't like your attitude, then look back at your philosophy— Rohn (1999)

3. **Your decisions determine whether you become unstoppable, not age, ethnic background, gender, economic class, where you grew up, the school you went to or didn't go to, past coaches, teachers, family, and the like.** Nor will talent, skills, knowledge, or experience ultimately decide your future or

fate. At the core of becoming an unstoppable game changer at whatever you do is the *right mindset*—a robust personal philosophy—not your natural gifts, birth year, birth order, birthright, or birthplace. It goes back to decisions, not conditions, because your daily decisions determine what you do with your talent, skills, knowledge, and experience.

"A man is literally what he thinks, his character being the complete sum of all his thoughts."—James Allen (AZ Quotes 2017)

Marisa Mills is the owner of Mills Automotive Group, RADCO Accessories Centers, Body Works, and other related businesses spread throughout the state of Minnesota. The Mills organizations create an incredible experience for both team members and customers, which can largely be attributed to their values-driven culture and their rigorous hiring and people-development processes. Mills and her executive team stay on a perpetual and relentless search for talent, both within and outside their organization. In her own words, here is an example of spotting the game changer traits at the periphery of an organization (take note that these traits can exist in people regardless of how young or old they may be).

Brady Sladek started with our Mills Automotive Group as a detailer—one who cleans up cars—at our Mills Ford of Brainerd dealership in July of 2000. He was working his way through college at the local community college here in Brainerd, Minnesota. At that time, I was also in the early stages of my positon—running, and being in charge of, our Mills Automotive Group, which consisted of six rooftops at that time. I officed at that time, and still do, out of our Mills Ford of Brainerd facility, and Brady was located in the same facility I was in. Very early on in his career with us, in August 2003, I was in my office working when Brady, this 19-year-old detailer, came and knocked on my door. Brady entered my office and informed me that he had been taking a college business class and part of the class requirement was to do an assessment, study, and paper on the business that he worked at. He was also to do the same assessment and study on the individual who ran the business. He was to assess strengths and weaknesses, positives and negatives, and opportunities for the business and the leader of this business. Part of his assignment was to share his assessment, observations, feedback, and suggestions with the leader of the business, which was, and still is, me. Brady was there to meet with me—to cover all the areas that he saw and assess what my business and I were doing good at and were not doing so good at.

I do not remember every detail of Brady's assessment that he went over with me; however, I do know and remember that the major takeaway for me (and ever since that moment to this day) was that I was hugely impressed! In the midst of that meeting, I absolutely knew that this kid had determination and ambition, was fearless, and had leadership qualities! The minute after he left my office, I got on the phone and had two of my sales managers for that store come into my office so that I could inform them of the awesome experience I had just had with Brady. They immediately came to my office and I told them about Brady's meeting with me. I instructed them to go back there, get that kid out of detail, and get a plan for Brady to be on the sales team in a way that was mutually beneficial for both him and us.

Within two weeks of that meeting, Brady was on the Mills Ford of Brainerd (MFB) sales team as a sales assistant. In four to five months, Brady earned a full-time MFB Sales Consultant position. Three years after that, Brady earned an F&I Manager (Finance and Insurance) position in that same dealership. Less than two years later, Brady earned a combined position of MFB Vehicle Sales Manager and F&I Manager at MFB. Less than two years later again, Brady had earned a New Vehicle Sales Manager position at MFB. Since 16 December 2011, Brady has been the General Sales Manager of MFB, which is our largest sales floor and sales team in a facility that we do not run with a general manager, because our executive team has offices there. Therefore, Brady is the key leader for the Mills Ford of Brainerd management team within our Automotive Group, where we have now grown to 15 rooftops, including five dealerships, a collision center, a wholesale parts distribution center, and an aftermarket accessories business.

Brady's ambition, hunger for more, drive, determination, and game changer mindset have continued to be at the helm of his professional career! He consistently runs an extremely disciplined, well-seasoned, and high-achieving team. There are so many things that I love and appreciate about Brady and his mindset. One of them is that over all the years, not everything has been easy for Brady professionally, yet he has always stayed the course, continued to energetically and mentally show up regardless of his circumstances, and committed and recommitted to being highly engaged and invested in his leadership position on my team! There are so many team members who have such great stories of how they became members on my team, developed themselves as team members, and continue to develop themselves on my team. Brady's story is one of my most beloved stories, because to a certain degree, Brady and I have grown up in this business together under the same roof. Watching and witnessing him, personally and professionally, are extremely inspiring to me, and it's also a reason that I know Brady will be successful no matter what he does (Marisa Mills, pers. comm.)!

Where do you find great people? Start with those you have! Sometimes the game changers you are looking for are right under your nose.

Speaking of up-and-coming game changers like Brady Sladek, it is becoming wearying to hear complaints about how lazy and entitled the new generation is today. For the most part, the people griping the most are the same melon-heads who raised their kids to be marshmallows. Kids are born today like they have always been, knowing nothing about anything. What they learn is what they are taught, and when weak-stick parents and school systems pamper them, entitle them, coddle them, and make life easy for them, it should not be a surprise when, as adults, they reflect lives that have been pampered, entitled, and coddled. We don't have an unfixable, deficit generation. We are reaping the consequences of deficit parenting that applied no consequences, didn't make kids earn it, and was more committed to their kids "having it better than we did" than they were loving them enough to let them struggle, endure pain and discomfort, and figure some things out on their own. Deep down, kids crave discipline and accountability, because nothing says, "I care about you" quite like accountability—"I care enough about you to make both of us uncomfortable in order to help you grow." Or, as my wife Rhonda would tell our Ashley when meting out appropriate consequences for actions, "I love you enough to let you hate me now." For too long, parents have ignored the timeless proverb: "A rod and a reprimand impart wisdom, but a child left undisciplined disgraces its mother"—Proverbs 29:15 (Biblica 2017).

But without discipline, having to earn it, and accountability, kids fail to develop the work ethic, habits, mental toughness, or character that would help them to become unstoppable as adults. To exacerbate matters, kids are pressured by social norms and peers to "fit in," which is, without question, one of life's surest routes to obscurity and mediocrity. Why fit in? Why? Most people, to a large degree, live uninspired, unimpressive, unaccomplished, and unfulfilled lives. Why fit in with that? Why not do what most others are *not* doing: starting earlier, working later, doing more than is required, setting your own pace, running your own race, and leveraging your own gifts and talents rather than trying to blend in with a mass of mediocrity? Arlington Independent School District's director of athletics, Kevin Ozee, puts it well: "In some cases, game changers are so rare and different that they are initially scoffed at for being out of the norm" (Kevin Ozee, pers. comm.).

The steel of greatness is forged in a pit, not by lounging in a hammock.

4. **Game changers are intensely competitive.** Yes, they compete intensely to continually *best* their former best, but those competitive instincts also translate into competing with others. Frankly, game changers want to win, love to win, and expect to win—every single time.

Coach Samar Azem at Campbell University observes:

They are competitive. They have an internal bar that they raise, meet, and repeatedly raise again with each challenge they seek out for themselves. It is an instinctive attribute that they habituate. What we see is the means to that process: a person who is always energetic and intense. What we don't see is that internally, that person is willful to win and be successful. And within their process, they're streamlining their energy to achieve whatever bar they've set for themselves, because they're knowledgeable of what it takes to succeed.

Simply put, the biggest attribute that differentiates the playmaker from the game changer is the level of competitiveness that the game changer has. If they have a high level of natural competitiveness, they know the process and will work at the process internally to succeed (Samar Azem, pers. comm.).

Horizon Forest Products executive David Williams adds, "They have a passion to 'WIN.' They absolutely want to be *FIRST*. They are not interested in what others are doing; they simply want to *WIN* more than everyone else" (David Williams, pers. comm.).

It is appropriate to point out that being competitive is a choice. It is something you decide you want to do. Competitiveness is not a rare gene that some are born with and others lack. It is formed from within, through mindset, decisions, and discipline.

Whit Ramonat, executive vice president of Penske Automotive, U.S. Marine, and a renowned no-nonsense, get-it-done leader, adds insight to the game changer philosophy this way: "From my observations and experience, game changers are driven to compete. They are also motivated by elements of fear and insecurity associated with failure. Their definition of failure is usually an internalized measure that a playmaker would consider success" (Whit Ramonat, pers. comm.).

Kevin Ozee suggests, "A game changer is a rare performer who breathes the thinnest of air. There are very few game changers in any field, and once you see them in action you can easily see the difference in the level of passion, loyalty, and commitment that they bring to their chosen endeavor. Specifically, game changers do not see anything other than winning and learning" (Kevin Ozee, pers. comm.).

"Winning is not everything, but wanting to win is."
—Vince Lombardi (b) (AZ Quotes 2017)

---

5. **Game changers demonstrate an energy and body language that introduces them to others long before they ever open their mouths.** Some team members slouch around the

workplace like Eeyore, the perennially depressed donkey friend of Winnie the Pooh—slumped shoulders, head down, feet shuffling along. They are energy-takers. You see them in athletics as well, slumped on the bench, disengaged and indifferent to what is taking place in the arena. As you may have already surmised, these are not game changers.

Game changers are energized by their goals, the chance to make a difference, the chance to lift a teammate, the chance to move the team forward, and the chance to be better today than they were yesterday. They do not require daily hugs or pep talks from peers or leaders. They have a consistent alertness and focus about them seen only sporadically among the other three performance groups. Ozee describes the game changer's presence well: "Game changers exude energy even without speaking. When they enter a room, you can sense the positive energy from a game changer. They are typically in good physical and mental health, and work hard to protect both" (Kevin Ozee, pers. comm.).

The Thermostat

Coach Beckner of Boise State explains the power of body language through the "thermostat" effect of the game changer: "When playmakers walk into a gym, they are thermometers. They take the temperature of the environment (competitiveness level, talent level, energy/emotion) and they adjust to it. They conform to the temperature. The game changer is a thermostat. He walks in the gym and *sets* the temperature. If the competitiveness level, talent level, or energy/emotion isn't where he likes it . . . he sets it. He demands, insists, and fights to have the gym and environment the way he wants them" (Phil Beckner, pers. comm.).

In just 11 years, Vertu Motors in the United Kingdom went from being a single automotive dealership to having over 130 locations. Vertu's CEO, Robert Forrester, is a fanatic for culture, values, positive energy, and "right fits" to grow his company. He is a hands-on leader who personally and regularly visits dealerships to take the culture's temperature. His correlation on the connection between performance and energy is clear and compelling:

> The key differentiator between an "A" player and a "C" player, other than talent, is the level of responsibility taken for their own personal performance and that of their team. This ranges from the drive to learn and get better to the extent to which they are willing to go the extra mile—drive and energy all come into it. The issue is "C" players never really become "A" players—they have something missing. I toured 20 dealerships between Christmas and the New Year, dropping in unannounced, and the variances were marked. In some places I was met with lethargy and excuses before I could say, "Hello." The quote "Excuses are the first exit on the highway of success" was never so true. "Turning up" was enough. In fact, in one dealership the management had not even turned up! The "A" players were bundles of energy and joy—spreading enthusiasm in their teams and creating energy and will to succeed. Success then breeds further success. My task as the leader coming away from this tour was twofold: to vow to get out of the office more and spend more time visiting the business itself, and secondly, to remove the "C" players (Robert Forrester, pers. comm.).

Energy is defined as "the strength and vitality required for sustained physical and mental activity" (Google 2017). You cannot teach energy, or even fake energy for long. You must hire it in and create the cultural conditions to bring it out, accelerate it, and sustain it.

It's About Focused Energy

The damage that undriven and lethargic people do to morale, momentum, the team member experience, the customer experience, the culture, and the brand is incalculable. And focused, positive cultural energy starts with leadership. The speed of the leader will determine the speed of the pack. Energized leaders—with or without official titles—can evoke energy from within others. But when the leader lets up a little, followers tend to let up a lot; when a leader catches a cold, the followers come down with pneumonia. Returning to the importance of philosophy, it goes a long way in determining the energy level, or apathy, of an individual. To upgrade your energy level, upgrade your philosophy.

Think about it. If your philosophy is that you are in control of your destiny as opposed to being that you are a victim, is it likely to impact your energy level positively? Absolutely!

If your philosophy is that you own your results and renounce excuses, will it impact energy and body language? Of course it will!

If your philosophy is to prove yourself over again today and *best* your former best—instead of borrowing credibility from past accomplishments—will it ward off complacency and drive higher energy levels? You know it!

If your philosophy is to blame your color, age, gender, ethnicity, lack of education, or bad breaks for your lack of success, will you have less positive energy than those who believe the power of their right daily decisions is what moves them to their potential? Without a doubt!

The game changer's definition of "bad luck" is the perfume of choice that losers spray to disguise the stench of their mediocrity, poor decisions, absent discipline, and anemic work ethic.

In summary, wherever you are in life right now is overwhelmingly the result of the decisions you made, and those decisions were based on your personal philosophy. Everyone has a philosophy, so that is neither the question nor the point. The questions are: Where is yours taking you? What habits has it created that are healthy or otherwise? Where has it put your daily attention? What has it caused you to overvalue that you should value less, and to disregard that you should focus more on?

Building a philosophy is an evolution based on experiences and maturation over time. But some folks grow older without growing wiser. Growth is never a guarantee. It must be intentional. That being said, creating a structured plan to reshape, revamp, or somehow strengthen your personal philosophy should be a high priority for anyone wanting to become unstoppable. Is it for you?

Mission Unstoppable

To become an unstoppable game changer, contemplate and take action on the following six points:

1. How can you improve your daily focus and consistency on what matters most so that you can stay on track longer, and recover faster when you veer off course?

2. What changes in thinking do you need to make to shed any "I'm a victim" mindset (which distracts you with external conditions you cannot control) and build an "I own it" philosophy (which keeps you zeroed in to improve and upgrade the aspects of your job and life you can directly control and affect)?

"Everything can be taken from a man but one thing: the last of the human freedoms—to choose one's attitude in any given set of circumstances, to choose one's own way."—Viktor E. Frankl (b) (AZ Quotes 2017)

3. Where have you been prone to blame "conditions," and what are those conditions? Identify three daily decisions that will marginalize the impact of adverse conditions.

"When we are no longer able to change a situation— we are challenged to change ourselves."—Viktor E. Frankl (a) (AZ Quotes 2017)

4. How can you compete more with your former self, and then translate those improvements to dominate your competition?

5. What do your body language and energy levels say about you? Are they positive only when things go your way? How can you change your thinking so you can change your energy and demonstrate powerful body language and energy levels even in adversity?

6. Use additional and helpful resources to help yourself and others create game changer performance. Visit www.JimRohn.com and sign up for Jim's free newsletter.

UNSTOPPA BULLET

"The greatest discovery of my generation is that a human being can alter his life by altering his attitudes."—William James (b) (AZ Quotes 2017)

CHAPTER 6

The Wonder of WHY

There is much wisdom in the words of Nietzsche: "He who has a why to live for can bear almost any how."
—Viktor E. Frankl (c), (AZ Quotes 2017)

Decades before Simon Sinek and Bill Hybels shared the power of "WHY" with multitudes through conferences and best-selling books, Nazi death camp survivor Viktor Frankl was explaining its power in his book *Man's Search for Meaning*. Frankl explained the wonder of WHY, which really is your reason—or reasons—for getting up each morning, and how it has incredible potential to power you through adversity, disappointments, setbacks, and hurts. It also has the ability to generate a drive and focus in you that the person with weaker or fewer reasons will lack. A WHY is personal, and thus it differs from one individual to another. There is not a right or a wrong WHY; there is *your* WHY. And as you can imagine, unstoppable game changers have a more compelling WHY that lesser performers lack. This is what prompts their focus, energy, effort, and resilience on a far more consistent basis than that of the playmaker, caretaker, or undertaker.

Sports performance specialist, author, and coach Allistair McCaw puts it this way: "I think after 23 years in the sports performance coaching game, my observation of what separates the occasionally better-than-average performer (the playmaker) from the team member who consistently brings effort, energy, and intensity day in and day out is that the champion athletes are more invested in the everyday grind and work. They not only have a passion for what they do, but they have a vision and greater purpose—a bigger 'WHY' if you like" (Allistair McCaw, pers. comm.).

Desire, Direction, Determination

Karate champion Johnny Gyro describes how desire, direction, and determination shaped his WHY to become the number-one-ranked fighter in the world:

> Speaking from my own personal experience, I have been successfully driven by three vital components, and they are: desire, direction, and determination. When I began my journey in the karate tournament fighting circuit starting in 1980, I had one clear desire in mind. My desire, and goal, was to become the number-one-rated fighter in the karate tournament national ratings system. It was a monumental task, to be sure; but it was achievable and possible, which was all the motivation I needed. I wanted to become an exceptional and extremely skillful fighter so that my name and reputation would be synonymous with victory. I was willing to do whatever it took to achieve that goal, knowing full well that it was not going to be easy to do. The reward to that achievement had nothing whatsoever to do with financial success or financial gain. This was not a money-driven goal, but a deep personal challenge. It was about achieving my personal best, and the only way to prove that would be to break records and set new ones. Having triumphed over all weight ranks and age groups, the true tale of success would be—and was solidified by—receiving recognition on the

pages of the most coveted, well-respected karate magazines and publications at that time, and then being featured on their covers. To achieve the fighting status and ranking that I dedicated myself to was a massive personal victory for me. To then make it into the record books where history is indelibly recorded was the ultimate realization of the goal that has provided me with gratifying and enduring satisfaction (Johnny Gyro, pers. comm.).

Without the focus that comes with a relevant and compelling WHY, you will drift from day to day being spread too thin and majoring in minor things—living a mile wide and an inch deep.

Your own WHY might be something as wide-ranging and could include factors such as these:

- To eat regularly and get a safer roof over my head.
- To move my family into a bigger house.
- To live in a mansion.
- To drive *that* vehicle.
- To attain *that* position.
- To be a starter on the team.
- To set *that* record.
- To help my sick mom.
- To provide food for orphans who cannot fend for themselves.
- To retire at *that* age.
- To be number one at *that*.
- To make *that* amount of money.

Basically, your WHY answers two questions: why you get up in the morning, and why anyone else should care that you get up in the morning. In other words, what do you want for yourself, and who can you help, impact, or elevate?

The Four Why's

Your WHY can normally be broken down into four components:

1. The survival component of WHY: the basic necessities you need to stay alive.
2. The material component of WHY: the possessions or physical assets and accolades (clothing, homes, jewelry, cars, boats, toys, investments, cash in the bank, gadgets, awards, rankings, recognition, and the like).
3. The external component of WHY: the people or causes you want to help, impact, add value to, and leave a legacy with.
4. The eternal component of WHY: the seeds you want to plant now—through your work, mentoring, financial contributions, and legacy—that will impact eternity.

The Survival Component of Why: Basic Necessities

I can recall that when I was just out of school and the business I worked in went broke, my WHY was basic—very basic. I moved into the only house I could afford, which happened to be infested with rats. I lived there a year. I had no furniture, and slept in a sleeping bag. My primary food was corn tortillas, because one of my three jobs that I took to work my way out of the tough time was delivering cases of corn tortillas to restaurants in the evening for 50 cents a case—and I got the damaged packages for free. I also sold two different products door-to-door. They were not at all ideal jobs, but I was happy to have them in an economy with 11 percent unemployment, 13 percent inflation, and 21 percent interest rates.

I worked day and night because my WHY was to move into a better place, eat better food, and buy some new clothes. While I have been blessed to move far beyond that stage in life, part of why I work so hard today is so I never return to that state. The survival aspect of my WHY still motivates me.

Alan Ram, president of Proactive Training Solutions, based in Phoenix, and an expert in management and telephone skills training, refers to the motivation that comes from "having no net"—a derivative of the survival aspect of WHY:

One of the attributes of many of the people I perceive to be game changers is that they live life without a net. While having loving and supporting parents is a wonderful thing, many of the most successful people I have known have a dysfunctional or minimal relationship with their parents. I'm not saying anyone should strive for that, but unfortunately not everyone has great parents. Sometimes, "it is what it is" can work to your advantage. Let me share how this applies to my story.

I still remember being 13 or 14 years old and exactly where I was standing in the kitchen as my father berated me and told my mother how I would never amount to anything—a story not unique to me, but impactful all the same. That kind of thing gets etched into a young man's psyche whether he wants it to be or not. Shortly after reaching the age of 16, I left an abusive home with really nowhere to go and no plan. I just knew I couldn't stay there. Fortunately, after a few days, I was taken in by the family of a friend who I lived with until I turned 17 and was old enough to join the United States Marine Corps.

I was far from the prototypical Marine recruit. I was a skinny 120-pound, 5′5″ Jewish kid from the suburbs of Buffalo who had never fired a weapon and was definitely no threat to end up on any recruiting poster. My size and lack of weapons skills going into this endeavor were definitely a disadvantage. The advantage I had was that I could not fail and return to Buffalo as a boot camp dropout. This was absolutely not an option because, if I didn't make it, I had no alternate plan after Uncle Sam. The days went by and as the training got tougher, more recruits would drop out. These were recruits coming in with superior physical and weapons skills compared to me, who, unfortunately for them, had the mental disadvantage afforded by the perceived luxury of a safety net. Many who would fall by the wayside would simply go home to their loving families to regroup and try something else. When the going got too tough and thoughts of supportive family and friends waiting at home became too hard to resist, it was just too easy to simply tap out. On a long and brutal forced march through the backwoods of Parris Island, it became very hard mentally for some to ignore the possibilities of their options. I had none other than to keep marching and enduring. I did not have the luxury of a safety net of people who would take care of me if I didn't succeed. Thinking back today, I am thrilled that I had no options, and I would not change a thing.

As life has gone on and as I have advanced my career in business, I have seen firsthand what the option of failure and always having that net to fall back on can do to someone's desire and persistence. Having spent much of my career in the automotive industry, I have seen hundreds of people with an abundance of talent fall by the wayside knowing they could always move back in with or seek the financial support of family if things didn't work out. Having that net in the back of one's mind can absolutely erode a "failure is not an option" mindset. Knowing with certainty that you can always go back is not something that will necessarily help you to succeed, nor a luxury you want or can afford. If you have a good relationship with your parents and family, congratulations. That is to be valued, and I am not suggesting anyone employ a "burn the boats" mindset with their families. What I am suggesting is that you value your relationships by not taking advantage of your family's (or friends') desire to protect you and provide you with that net should it be needed. You're not going to burn the boats, but mentally you want to tell yourself every day that those boats have sailed on to a different port, never to return. Wake up every day convincing yourself that failure is not an option and there's no going back. Tell yourself you have no net until you believe it. Don't let the thought of a safety net make you soft in your desire, because it will. It's up to you to make it on your own and make every opportunity you have to succeed count (Alan Ram, pers. comm.).

As Alan points out, it is ironic how sometimes the traumatic events in our lives help awaken, focus, and energize our talent, skills, and knowledge.

Adam Hermann is director of sports performance at Boise State University, and his explanation of this phenomenon is spot on:

> I have been fortunate enough to work with athletes across many disciplines in my career who were extremely talented. They were disciplined, detailed, and enthusiastic. They made plays to help win games and cared about their fellow teammates.
>
> These players are pretty common. Every team has one or two of these players—"playmakers." Every team needs playmakers to win games and be competitive. If a team has no playmakers, it is going to be tough to be competitive, let alone win games.
>
> I have also been fortunate enough in my career to be a part of many championship teams in many different sports. All those championship teams had playmakers on their roster. But the biggest difference between a championship team and a good team is the "game changer." A game changer is someone who brings a level of intensity, effort, attitude, discipline, and accountability unmatched by anyone else on the team, and, in doing so, raises the standards and the habits of the entire organization in the process. These are the type of people that championships are won with. These are overachievers.
>
> I have spent my entire professional career as a sports performance coach at the "mid-major" level. I have never had a blue-chip recruit walk through our doors. We have never had anyone that showed up as a freshman and was ready to be "the" guy. Every player I have worked with who has become a game changer was developed into that type of person by a combination of his personality and the development we put into him physically, mentally, and emotionally.
>
> So what makes someone a game changer rather than a playmaker? In my opinion, and from my experience, it is trauma. Talent needs trauma. When the talented athlete has faced

trauma and overcomes that trauma, this can lead to high achievement. We call them overachievers because they have overcome something in order to achieve at a high level. That trauma can come from childhood experiences or social experiences that they have encountered in their lives. The following are two different examples of talented basketball players who faced their own trauma growing up and used that experience to push and drive them to become an overachiever and a game changer.

Derrick Marks was a playmaker for our men's basketball team as a freshman, sophomore, and junior. He had a good but tough upbringing in the city of Chicago. He overcame early trauma in his childhood life to eventually earn a full scholarship to play NCAA Division I basketball. He had been an all-conference player on a good team that won a lot of games. But up until the summer going into his senior year, that was about it. Then trauma hit. Derrick tore the meniscus in his knee and opted to have it repaired, which meant he would be laid up, unable to walk, run, or play basketball for nearly three months. With the biggest summer of his career right around the corner, he would not be able to train, practice, lift, and run with his team. What would he do? Derrick was never known as a great shooter; he was more of a driver and scorer.

So after his surgery, while he couldn't even stand up without the use of crutches, he was in a gym, sitting in a chair, and making shot after shot. Soon he could stand, and he continued to make shot after shot, sometimes up to 1,000 makes a day. He attacked his rehab with discipline and urgency, and kept making shot after shot while he watched his teammates play open gym. Eventually Derrick returned to full status in October. What happened after that was the stuff of a game changer. Derrick led his team to the regular season championship and an at-large bid into the NCAA tourney while being named the conference player of the year. He averaged career highs in points and three-point field goal percentage, and he was the one we looked to at the end of games. He carried this team and made everyone around him better in the process. Derrick was a talented player who faced trauma at the right time in his career and, because of it, he overcame and became a game changer.

Rob Heyer was a basketball player that nobody wanted. Not much basketball talent comes out of the state of Wyoming, and Rob seemed to be just another guy. He attended a junior college out of high school and played there for two years. After his junior college playing days were over, the best offer he received to continue playing basketball was at a small Division II school in the middle of Texas, and a bad program at that. Rob moved to Texas and spent a year at that school, playing sparingly on an average team. After one year, Rob decided to leave. His mom lived in Boise, Idaho, and he decided he would transfer to Boise State and be a walk-on to the basketball team. Rob had to sit a year due to NCAA transfer rules, which meant he could only practice with the team and then would have only one year to play. During the early months of Rob's first year at Boise State, he broke his ankle and it required surgery. So before practice even started he was out for the year. How would he have a chance to show what he could do?

There was a lot of trauma facing Rob—from his past, and now his current injury situation. Rob had surgery and started rehab determined to make it back. He spent that year watching practice from the sidelines and eventually running stairs during practice once he was cleared for it.

Going into his senior year, Rob's ankle was healed and he was ready to try to be a contributing part of this team. One problem was that the coaches barely even knew his name, and no one thought he could be a player. As summer workouts began and fall practice started, one thing kept becoming clear every day: Rob's effort, attitude, and work ethic consistently stood out, and his teammates were starting to see him as a leader. All of a sudden, Rob had made an impact because of his work ethic, and he raised the level of everyone around him. He found a place on the floor that year, and was the sixth man on a conference championship and NCAA tourney team. Rob was a game changer. He made everyone around him better by raising the expectations for how we would work and prepare as a team. He overcame trauma and was an integral part of a championship team because of it.

Not every game changer I have been around has had to overcome early setbacks or injuries to become a game changer. But there has never been a game changer in my career who has not had to overcome some form of trauma. This is where the coach comes in. When a talented playmaker arrives on campus and has never faced any real adversity or had to overcome any real trauma, it is the job of the coach to apply that trauma in a calculated and methodical way to take that playmaker and see whether he has what it takes to become a game changer. This is where the coach can be invaluable. The coach can take that athlete to the next level. Not every athlete is willing or able to overcome the trauma that a coach applies, and the coach must know which athletes have the capability to overcome the trauma and transform themselves into something beyond playmaker. There is an art to this coaching that comes through experience and building a relationship with the athlete.

I have been around game changers who came from great families and were afforded everything they needed in life up until that point. They had never truly faced any adversity; therefore, they never had to overcome anything where they faced some real trauma in their lives. Once the coach applied that trauma to them, they showed their true resiliency and overcame that trauma to lead their teams to championships. The role of the coach in the game changer cannot be overlooked.

I think it is also important to note that just because someone has overcome some trauma in his life does not guarantee he will develop into a game changer. But without it, it is as close to a guarantee as there is that he will not develop into one (Adam Hermann, pers. comm.).

Talent without toughness is unrefined. Toughness without talent is frustrating. Talent with toughness can become unstoppable.

The Material Component of WHY: Possessions and Accolades

The material can be very motivating, but if it dominates your WHY, you can begin to live a very shallow and selfish life. I can recall a stage in my life where most of my material WHYs began with the letter *B*. I wanted: a book deal, a business, a beach house, a Bentley, a Black Card, a black belt, and the like. Over time, I have been blessed with all of them, and still enjoy what is in the material category and material goals; but my primary focus has shifted more heavily to the external and eternal—a reminder of how essential it is to keep your WHY relevant and compelling.

Working hard and earning nice possessions is a just reward. But do not let the possessions possess you. Don't just make money; make a difference.

The External Component of WHY: People or Causes

EasyCare, a company with hundreds of employees, based in Atlanta, is dedicated to helping car dealers create more passionate and engaged employees and customers. Its CEO, Larry Dorfman, articulates the external component of his WHY well:

I believe what most separates playmakers from game changers is their WHY. Those driven by only the results of the work frequently see it all as "work," whereas those who find a greater cause in what they do see it as part of their lives and have a different kind of passion and engagement in the process.

It's not about a win or loss; it is about an overall impact. For me personally, it is all about helping others succeed. This isn't just at the job, but it's every day in life. As Dave Anderson says, "Every day means every day." The only way I believe someone does something "every day" is to really find purpose in that thing they do, and to adopt it as a part of their way of life (Larry Dorfman, pers. comm.).

> **"People who live for themselves are in a mighty small business." —John Maxwell (2005)**

The Eternal Component of WHY: Seeds You Want to Plant

Your WHY will change as your life evolves and your goals change, and as you adjust priorities. It is essential that you keep your WHY relevant and compelling in a way that breathes fresh purpose into every day, and fuels the fire daily to make you unstoppable. One danger that many fail to realize is that as they successfully attain their dreams and scratch items off their WHY list, their reasons can become smaller, and their daily fight less tenacious. Thus, it is essential to continue to refine and define your WHY—to consistently stretch your dreams to keep your WHY and its ensuring hunger impactful on a daily basis.

> **As prosperity rises, urgency, hunger, work ethic, and intensity are prone to fall.**

Using Doubt and Disrespect

Your WHY may also be impacted by outside forces such as:

- Someone who believes in you, stood by you, or invested in you, and you do not want to let him or her down.

- Those who doubt you, disrespect you, or dismiss you, and you want to prove they are wrong.

Oliver Maroney was raised in Portland, Oregon, and has developed relationships with numerous influential performers and leaders as the senior sportswriter for *Dime* magazine. He has used the doubts that others have of him to elevate his motivation, rather than become devastated or discouraged:

The pressure people put on themselves varies from person to person. You always hear players talk about having no bigger critic than themselves. I think that ideology is very true. The players who hold themselves to a higher standard than those around them not only perform better, but work harder as well. They set goals that are almost unachievable, knowing that, while they may not meet their goals, falling short isn't really failing. People with outside motivation—using the doubts or words of others—also seem to thrive in producing results and accomplishing more. They want to prove others wrong and continue to do so, no matter how hard they have to work. What's most interesting to me is the number of people that don't have that killer instinct or drive. I'm talking about the people who settle for less or don't set the bar higher. Whether it's playing on the basketball court or writing a story, it always seems like the person who has that outside motivation to succeed works harder, and, in turn, wins.

My entire career I've been doubted. I didn't have many friends in high school, and I was always trying to prove others wrong, whether it be in the classroom or elsewhere. I wanted people to realize that I was somebody; and, most importantly, I wanted to be taken seriously. I got a job when I was 15 and a half. I had good grades, and I worked harder than anyone I knew. I always filled my free time with workouts, projects, or work because I didn't want to fall behind on my goals. It was frustrating when I didn't get the attention I felt I had deserved. What drove me to do this was my motivation to prove others wrong. I didn't want to look back on life and say, "Well, I didn't do my best." Instead, I wanted to say, "See, I proved you wrong." In everything I did from middle school on, I approached doubt as a challenge. I wanted to go out and prove myself to everyone who doubted me. To this day, I still use that as motivation. People tell me I look "too young" and, instead of getting down or upset, I use that to my advantage. If I let someone tell me that and I get upset, sad, or disappointed, I've now let that person win. So I used other people's negativity or questions about me as fuel to my fire. I don't think I'll ever be satisfied with my life, because I always want to be the best. In order to be the best, I think you have to possess a focus, mentality, and belief that you're better than what others say (Oliver Maroney, pers. comm.).

Like Maroney, National Basketball Association (NBA) star Damian Lillard uses the doubts and disrespect of others to intensify his WHY. His off-season coach, Phil Beckner, relates how Lillard was just a two-star recruit out of high school and chose to go to Weber State, where he was named conference MVP two times and elevated his performance to become an NBA lottery pick (number six with the Portland Trail Blazers).

Lillard had a fire burning inside him to put Weber State on the map, as well as to make his dreams of becoming an NBA player a reality. Beckner describes how Lillard referred to disparaging remarks, doubts, and disrespect he received during his journey as "wood on the fire"—borrowing from Michael Jordan's retirement speech. Lillard also uses the hashtag "#NGE"—not good enough—in social media when an incident warrants it. For example, after earning the accolades of rookie of the year and two-time all-star, but then being selected to only the second team All-NBA, Lillard used the hashtag #NGE on Twitter to announce his second team inclusion (Phil Beckner, pers. comm.). Lillard uses factors others would be demoralized by to intensify his work ethic, hunger, and focus.

UNSTOPPA
BULLET

"A successful man is one who can lay a firm foundation with the bricks others have thrown at him." —David Brinkley (AZ Quotes 2017)

In summary, your WHY gives you purpose and focus, and builds persistence and resilience that can make you unstoppable. People with both more and compelling reasons do not quit; they fight. And when they hit walls, they bounce; they do not splatter. Here is a friendly wake-up call: It is no one else's responsibility to make you hungry or to convince you to "want it." That, dear reader, is on *you*. That being said, what will you do right now to put the wonder of WHY to work for you?

Mission Unstoppable

To become an unstoppable game changer, you will need to consider and take action on the following five key points:

1. Considering the four components of WHY listed in this chapter, as well as the outside forces others say or do that motivate you, what is your WHY?

2. Is your WHY specific enough to measure and quantify? Is it specific enough for you to know whether you are currently winning or losing, or if you will ultimately win or lose?

3. Is your WHY in writing somewhere so that you can review it as part of your morning mindset routine to help increase focus and purpose for each day?

4. What did your WHY make you do yesterday that you would not have done if you did not have a WHY? What is it making you do today for the same effect? If you cannot be specific, your WHY may not be compelling enough.

5. Use additional and helpful resources to help yourself and others create game changer performance. Attend the Mission Unstoppable three-day seminar at our Elite Center near Los

Angeles. For more details, visit the events page at www
.LearnToLead.com.

You will lose your way when you lose your WHY. You
will find yourself as you pursue it with all that you have
to give every day.

Live Your Life in the Zone

The lie of "focus" is that it always helps you to perform better. The truth is that focus can destroy your potential if you are focused on the wrong things. Only a focus that enables peak performance is to be desired and pursued.

In athletics, it is common to refer to someone as being "in the zone." The pitcher who doesn't allow a hit or walk a batter, the quarterback with 15 straight completions, the golfer who plays a flawless round, or the point guard who hits five straight three-point shots are all examples of being in the zone. But the zone is not reserved for sports alone. Regardless of what we do, there is a zone that makes us far more effective when we find it, stay in it, and return to it quickly if we depart.

"Zone," in the context of this chapter, can be defined as *a temporary state of heightened focus that enables peak performance*. Notice the *temporary* aspect. No one is always so consistently and unflinchingly focused that he or she never leaves the zone. To become unstoppable, we need to focus on three primary aspects in relation to the zone:

1. Getting in it more often.
2. Staying in it longer.
3. When we leave it, recovering and returning to it faster.

Also, notice in the definition the qualifier for focus—that it is the kind of focus that enables peak performance. This is where you are at your best and performing optimally. As pointed out previously, not all focus is helpful; in fact, a relentless focus on trivial things, matters beyond your control, blame, excuses, or concern over what someone else is doing or how you are measuring up to others is a destructive focus that completely derails your potential.

Focus is defined as the ability to concentrate. Whether or not you reach a point where unstoppable game changer status dominates your life depends greatly upon *what* you are concentrating on day in and day out.

A Momentum Maker

Momentum is defined as a "force that allows something to continue or to grow stronger or faster as time passes" (Merriam-Webster 2017). Based on that definition, focus can be one heck of a momentum maker when you are in the zone and focusing on the most productive thoughts and actions! Focus, the ability to concentrate, is a force that allows productive things to continue, grow faster, and grow stronger over time—if you are focused on the right things to begin with. The opposite is also true. Without a focus on the right things, do you really have any positive momentum at all? Not a chance. You may have negative momentum, as evidenced by having the wrong things continuing and growing faster and stronger when you are focused on unproductive activities. But this is not the kind of momentum you need to become unstoppable. The lesson is simple: If you want more positive daily momentum, you will need to spend more time in the zone, focusing on the thoughts and actions most predictive of achieving your goals and becoming unstoppable.

UNSTOPPA BULLET

You cannot passively wait for momentum, just hoping it shows up. You must create it. *Positive momentum is earned!*

Aspire for "Good Used Up"

Without question, when you are performing from within your zone and benefiting from momentum, you feel it: Time flies by, work is fun, you feel powerful and in control, energy and momentum are high, and at day's end you feel fulfilled. Equally certain is the fact that you feel it just as strongly when you are working outside of your zone: you are always playing catch-up, you play to maintain, you feel overwhelmed, and at the end of the day you wonder what exactly you accomplished.

One of my personal daily affirmations is to be "totally used up at the end of each day." In other words, I want to give it my all, every single day and without exception. This is not just at work, but in every sphere of life: relationships, spiritually, mentally, all of it. But I have found that there are two types of being "used up"—a good used up and a bad used up.

With the "good used up" you are completely drained at day's end, but you still feel fulfilled because you know that you did what mattered, made a difference, stuck to your disciplines, stayed in attack mode, and planted seeds for a better tomorrow. At the end of the day you find a quiet place, kick back, reflect, and sip that 24-year-old bourbon, neat, relishing the day's progress and impact.

With the "bad used up," you are still completely drained but you feel unsettled rather than fulfilled. You wonder what you accomplished, your mind is blurry, and you have regrets. And you can forget about the 24-year-old bourbon; you're tossing back the equivalent of moonshine trying to deaden the reality that in the past 24 hours you may have even taken a step backward, and are further from your dreams than when the day began.

 Direction is more important than speed, progress more relevant than motion, and accomplishment more vital than activity.

It's About Effort

Boise State's Adam Hermann paints a poignant picture of the in-the-zone game changer who is destined to chalk up a win in the "good used up" column at day's end:

> Game changers bring their best effort to work each and every day. How do we define effort? We define effort as enthusiasm, focus, finish, opportunity, resilient, and together.
>
> Game changers bring a genuine enthusiasm to whatever it is they do, because they are excited about the opportunity to get better and to compete. A game changer has a laser focus that locks in on the task at hand (whether that is practice, film study, or a game) and helps others stay focused as well. Game changers finish everything they start. They view the act of finishing as a mindset and a way of life. They are finishers. They get stronger as the game goes on. Game changers are opportunistic. They take advantage of every opportunity to get better, and they see opportunities all around them. They know that if they take advantage of all those opportunities, then when the big opportunity of competition presents itself, they will be ready. Game changers are resilient. They have had to overcome trauma and adversity in their lives and they have bounced back from it. They embrace adversity, because they know they will grow stronger because of it. Finally, game changers bring people together. They solidify a team and help them go places they never thought they could because they are

not afraid to sacrifice themselves for the greater good of the team.

If you take the first letter from each of those characteristics—Enthusiasm, Focus, Finish, Opportunity, Resilient, Together—that gives you the definition of *EFFORT*. That is what being a game changer is all about (Adam Hermann, pers. comm.).

And I would add that is also what being in the zone is all about. In fact, this is why Chapter 6 on "The Wonder of WHY" precedes this chapter—experience has shown that the clearer you are about what matters most in your life and what you are fighting for each day, the less likely you are to take as many or as lengthy detours out of your zone pursuing what does not achieve that end.

Be More Impervious to Distractions

Coach Phil Beckner has intensively coached and trained the Portland Trail Blazers' Damian Lillard for eight years. He continues to work with him over a two-week period in the summer off-seasons, both in Utah and in Boise, for two workouts a day (a skills workout and a shooting workout). On one occasion Beckner accompanied Lillard to train him each day during a 15-day Adidas tour covering Japan, China, and Paris. After working out for the first three days, on an early morning in the reserved gym, the Adidas rep from Japan asked Beckner if Lillard always worked out so hard. Beckner told him, "No. Usually he does two per day, but with other obligations on the trip we've narrowed it to just once" (Phil Beckner, pers. comm.).

Beckner describes how the unstoppable Lillard stayed in the zone on this trip around the world despite demands and distractions aplenty: "On day 11, we were going to fly from China to Paris, and Lillard asked, 'What time are we working out?'"

To this, Beckner replied, "You need a day off. If you work out I'm going home." Lillard conceded.

Beckner continues,

We leave China at midnight to fly to Paris (a 12-hour flight) and land at 7:30 AM in Paris. Dame takes two National Basketball Association (NBA) balls with him on the flight, and keeps them in the compartment above his seat. Upon landing, he opens the cabinet and asks, "When are we working out?" We went right to the hotel and then to the gym. He worked out, and had the best workout of the journey. He made 85 percent of his shots. He didn't want to rest or wait; he wanted to work. No one, and nothing, took him out of his zone the whole trip. And he was maintaining this hunger, drive, and unstoppable work ethic after he had already been a two-time NBA All-Star and Rookie of the Year (Phil Beckner, pers. comm.).

In addition, I can personally attest to Lillard's persistent hunger to become better, based on a one-hour phone conversation in which I explained to him the "stay hungry with a red belt mindset" concept I had presented in my book *It's Not Rocket Science: Four Simple Strategies for Mastering the Art of Execution*. Here it was, one evening in the off-season—when most guys are partying or lounging—and Lillard wanted insight and advice on how to stay even hungrier and more intense. I assure you, I learned more from *him* during that conversation than he learned from me. (I also discovered he raps with the same excellence and intensity he plays with, and recommend his album, *The Letter O*. I especially like "Loyal to the Soil.")

> The unstoppable game changer seeks to daily make his or her "temporary state of heightened focus" less temporary.

Beware "Zone Busters"

It stands to reason that if peak performance requires that we be in the zone with a heightened state of focus, then we should endeavor daily—and throughout each day—to engage in what creates that focus and to avoid what destroys it. This increased awareness is a key trait that separates the occasional playmaker who is focused *sometimes* from the unstoppable game changer who brings the focus, energy, and enthusiasm day in and day out (the person who gets off track less often, and stays off track for lesser amounts of time). Following is an extensive sample list of "in the zone" mindsets and actions, as well as zone busters (mindsets and actions that lessen or destroy focus and temporarily take you or keep you out of your zone). Unstoppable people are not flawless, but they develop significantly far more awareness of the mindsets and actions that optimize performance, and invest daily effort to avoid those that inhibit or destroy it.

"In the Zone" Mindsets and Actions	Zone Busters
Focusing on what you can control.	Focusing on external conditions you can't control.
Accepting responsibility; owning it.	Blaming or making excuses.
Choosing a positive attitude.	Choosing a negative attitude.
Being solution-focused.	Being problem-focused; complaining.
Using uplifting language.	Using "can't do" language, gossiping, or whining.
Overlooking what doesn't matter.	Choosing to be offended.
Planning and preparation.	Winging it; making things up as you go along.
Practicing.	Engaging in mindless, trivial activities.
Looking for possibilities.	Looking for scapegoats.
Following the process.	Cheating the process; skipping steps.
Being honest and full of integrity.	Lying, deceiving, and spinning the truth.
Choosing to grow.	Choosing to remain as you are.
Associating with uplifting people.	Associating with lazy, negative, divisive, or whining people.

(*Continued*)

"In the Zone" Mindsets and Actions	Zone Busters
Listening to feedback.	Tuning out feedback without even considering it.
Developing through self-improvement books, CDs, and the like.	Being absorbed in excess media, social media, and trash TV and publications.
Being a giver.	Being a manipulator or taker.
Being team-focused.	Being selfish; infected with the "disease of me."
Deciding up front what matters most.	Having too many goals or unclear priorities.
Forgiving and moving on.	Holding grudges and wanting to get even.
Reconciling and moving on.	Holding on to bitterness and hate.
Embracing accountability.	Failing to hold oneself or others accountable.
Having humility.	Boasting; being prideful or arrogant.
Focusing on being your best every day.	Tirelessly trying to win the approval of others.
Seeing "failure" as feedback.	Seeing failure as failure.
Seeing rejection as engagement.	Seeing rejection as personal or final.
Feeding your mind faithful thoughts.	Feeding your mind fearful thoughts.
Rehearsing what went right.	Dwelling on what went poorly.
Focusing on what is in front of you.	Focusing on what is behind or around you.
Obsessing to be your best.	Obsessing with how others are doing.
Being happy for others.	Being resentful of others.
Looking for what is good in someone.	Looking for what is bad in someone.
Maintaining a sense of gratitude.	Maintaining a sense of entitlement.
Keeping commitments.	Breaking commitments.

(*Continued*)

"In the Zone" Mindsets and Actions	Zone Busters
Having a clear conscience.	Having a guilty conscience.
Having faith.	Dreading what hasn't happened yet and may not.
Encouraging someone.	Putting others down.
Exhibiting kindness and respect.	Exhibiting rudeness or disrespect.
Seeking to understand.	Judging and condemning.
Choosing to be accepting.	Choosing to be prejudicial.
Assuming or expecting the best.	Assuming or expecting the worst.
Cultivating consistency.	Cultivating inconsistency.
Developing discipline.	Seeking instant gratification.
Choosing courtesy.	Being defensive.
Possessing strong body language.	Possessing weak body language.
Engaging in conversations about productive action.	Engaging in conversations about reality TV, fantasy football, and the like.
Focusing on being better today.	Having concern over measuring up to others.
Seeking and embracing coaching.	Seeking to prove you are right.
Overlooking trivial matters that don't derail your destiny.	Fighting every battle.
Doing what's right.	Trying to please everyone.
Taking wrong thoughts captive and remaining silent.	Impulsively blurting out stupidities that you later regret.

There is an unmistakable and indisputable correlation between your ability to stay in the zone and your progress on the journey to become unstoppable.

Fodder for Right Philosophy

In Chapter 5 when I presented the concept that your personal philosophy has the power to turn you into a victim, to make you unstoppable, or to put you somewhere in between, I suggested that if you want to change your results—and change your life—you would first need to change your philosophy. The preceding "in the zone" versus zone buster mindsets and actions offer a buffet of philosophies that you can choose to embrace or discard as you endeavor to refine your own philosophy in a manner that enables unstoppable game changer status to dominate your personal life and work life.

Don't Take the Bait!

Perhaps one of the most common zone busters of those listed is the propensity of choosing to take offense at what someone else says or does.

No one, and nothing, can offend you without your consent. You must choose to take offense—to take the bait and step out of your zone without knowing if, or when, you will return.

Sadly, I have seen people arrive at work and complain about the "idiot that cut me off in traffic" from nine in the morning until lunchtime. I cannot help but wonder, if it is so easy to get inside that person's head, how he or she can possibly win at anything. I would relish competing against someone so mentally inept who would shift his or her limited and precious energy and focus into something so utterly meaningless in the overall scope of one's life, especially in relation to how minuscule a bearing it has on reaching one's potential. To exacerbate matters, we are living in an age of offenses. Fueled by the swelling stench of political correctness that has shaped the snowflake culture we live in, people have found it far too easy to take offense today, to become victims, and to depart from the zone they need to remain in to become unstoppable. Following is a mercifully brief snapshot of examples (some of which you may be able to relate to, but will, one hopes, outgrow by the time you have finished this book):

- You post a political comment on social media and are surprised when others disagree. You then enter a prolonged debate about who is right that devolves into name-calling and worse. At this point you are so far out of your zone that you are unlikely to find your way back that day or in the subsequent days, as your need to be right and have the last word trumps your need to be unstoppable.

- A server in a restaurant does not refill your tea fast enough, or at all, and you begin picking apart everything about the service, and disparage all you find substandard about the establishment overall.

- You post a photo on Facebook and get only three "likes." Then you pout and continue to post even more photos until someone pays you the notice you feel is your due—which they don't. So then you sink into depression, and resolve to get even by not liking anyone else's photos.

- Someone talks too loudly, moves too slowly, drives too fast, does not say "please," laughs at your tie, ignores your new hairdo, interrupts you, bumps into you, disses your football team, ignores your kids, gives someone else too much credit, gives you too little, is overpaid, and the march of misery continues ad infinitum—as does the time you spend out of your zone fretting about what often amounts to a load of garbage—absolute garbage. I mean, really, in the overall scope of your life and in relation to the bearing it has on you reaching your fullest potential as a human being, how much time, energy, and emotion will you continue to give to incidental nonsense that does not really matter?

I am not suggesting that you become a doormat; not in the least. But when you think about how much mental focus you are prone to give to what is mostly trivial, it is probably embarrassing. You are offended? *So what?* Nothing happens: nothing! Show me the bruises and blood. Did you go blind or lame? Did it maim you? No? Then, in the words of Larry Winget from the title of his 2004 book, *Shut Up, Stop Whining, and Get a Life.* And if you get damaged emotionally by someone's actions on social media, then stay off social media. If people like Bill Maher cause you distress, then stop watching Bill Maher. It frees you and focuses you on what matters most when you give up entering every debate, putting everyone in their place, and proving everyone else wrong. Want to be unstoppable? Renounce that nonsense, get back in your zone, shift into unstoppable game changer gear, and chase down those dreams. Unless the someone or something you are prone to take offense at is paying rent for the space it's consuming in your head, evict it and move on.

"The art of being wise is the art of knowing what to overlook." —William James (a) (AZ Quotes 2017)

The 4 C's of in-the-Zone Performance

Jeff Janssen, of the renowned Janssen Sports Leadership Center, talks often about the 4 C's for effective performance, all of which are about being in the zone:

> In our Leadership Academies, we talk all the time about the importance of the 4 C's for being an effective performer and Leader by Example. The "Best of the Best" learn and master the 4 C's: commitment, confidence, composure, and character.
>
> **Commitment:** A person's commitment level has a *huge* impact on his or her success. We have created a tool called the Commitment Continuum, which outlines seven different levels of commitment that people can show toward a task, team, or cause. The seven levels are: resistant, reluctant, existent, compliant, committed, compelled, obsessed. The

best performers realize that commitment is a choice, and they choose to consistently bring it at the committed or compelled levels. They invest themselves fully in whatever they do and seek to take others along with them.

Confidence: Successful people also have confidence in their abilities. This confidence is earned by diligently training and preparing at a committed or compelled level. Once this foundation is in place, confidence is then chosen by focusing on one's particular strengths, past successes, preparation, and praise given to them by others. We call these the four sources of confidence and encourage people to focus on them whenever they need to build their own confidence, or the confidence of a teammate. Despite adversity, failure, and critics, successful people overcome their fears, trust their training and preparation, and confidently take on challenges by developing and dwelling on their four sources of confidence.

Composure: Virtually anyone can succeed in low-pressure situations when there are few distractions and little is on the line. However, successful people perform at a high level under pressure. They produce consistent, high-level results under high-stress conditions. They know how to manage their emotions and stay calm, cool, and collected during crunch time. They do this by controlling the controllables: their attitude, effort, preparation, and so forth. They also focus intently on the present moment and on the positive things they want to do versus the negative things they want to avoid, and take care of the process that leads to the outcome they want. Their poise under pressure not only helps them be successful—it sends a positive ripple effect to the rest of the team that helps them stay calm and composed as well.

Character: Finally, successful people compete and represent their teams with character. They compete with class and refuse to cheat or take shortcuts. They know that sustainable success depends on their ability to consistently do the right thing, even when, and especially when, no one is watching. They aren't willing to sacrifice their integrity for hollow, short-term gains. Their definition of success transcends mere wins and losses; it also incorporates the kind of person they want to be, the impact they want to have, and the legacy they want to leave.

The 4 C's (commitment, confidence, composure, character) are what differentiate the best performers. They work in every arena, whether it is sports, school, business, or life (Jeff Janssen, pers. comm.).

Speaking of how right character keeps you in the zone, Allistair McCaw adds, "However, one of the greatest contributions from a high performer or champion athlete is their character. They are people you can rely on and count on, no matter what the score or situation. They are always accountable, trustworthy, and loyal to their teammates and coaches, as well as the team's standards and values" (Allistair McCaw, pers. comm.).

The zone is real. You know when you are in it and when you are not. You know what puts you in it and what takes you out. The rest is up to you.

In summary, the zone is a temporary state of heightened focus that enables peak performance. To become an unstoppable game changer, your objective is to make that state less temporary, and to understand what puts you in the zone, as well as the zone busters that focus you on the wrong things and make peak performance impossible. And, most important, *you* get to choose how much time you will spend in and out of the zone each day. No one can exile you out of your zone. No one is blocking your path to get in, and no one and nothing can take you out unless *you* let it. You will take the bait from time to time. You will get distracted. You will major in minor things, let up, pursue the trivial rather than the essential, and have emergencies of the moment that break your focus for longer than they should. But you cannot let it happen very often, or for very long, if you are truly committed to becoming unstoppable.

Mission Unstoppable

To become an unstoppable game changer, consider and act on the following:

1. Which zone busters must you give up in order to go up to unstoppable game changer status? Review the list again and place a check mark by those you engage in too often. Become more aware of taking the bait, and measure your growth by your progress in taking it less often, and regrouping faster and returning to your zone after you depart.

2. Consider how much more effective you would be if you could spend 10, 20, 30 (or more) percent of your time in your zone with a heightened state of focus that enables peak performance. Where would you be today had you been more aware of this and made appropriate adjustments one, five, 10, 50 years ago? While you cannot go back and start over again from the beginning, you can start over now and make a new end—an end that results in having game changer status dominate your personal and professional life.

   Again, none of us will attain perfection, but the words of Vince Lombardi should encourage us to strive for it nonetheless:

UNSTOPPA *BULLET*

> **"Perfection is not attainable, but if we chase perfection we can catch excellence"** —Vince Lombardi (a) (AZ Quotes 2017)

3. Create more awareness for your team by conducting a meeting and diagramming on a whiteboard the "In the Zone" versus "Zone Busters" lists. Be sure to have team members participate.

4. Begin to consider now what you can do before you get to work (or on the way to work) that will put you in your zone before you arrive there. There is guidance on this discipline in Chapter 11.

5. Use additional and helpful resources to help yourself and others create game changer performance. Watch the DVD I created on the topic, *How to Stay in Your Execution Zone*, available at www. LearnToLead.com.

Everyone focuses on something and is consistent in some things. What you focus on and are consistent with determines how much time you spend in your zone, and how often you live your life in game changer status.

CHAPTER 8

Go A.P.E.!

Someone can help you become more than you are, but no one can make you something you are not. You can help others become more than they are, but you cannot make them something they are not.

Attitude, passion, and enthusiasm (A.P.E.) are "inside jobs." While one person may alter the mood of another based on how the first person treats the second, one's prevailing attitude, passion, and enthusiasm start from *within*. They are also critical success factors that help lift one to unstoppable status. The quality and level of your attitude, passion, and enthusiasm will also depend greatly on principles we discussed in the past two chapters. If your WHY is compelling, and you consciously spend more time in your zone with a heightened state of focus, your attitude, passion, and enthusiasm will become accelerated.

Lesser performers require excessive external stimulation to elevate their attitude, passion, and enthusiasm. It seems every day they need to be hugged, burped, coddled, cajoled, begged, bribed, or pumped up in order to deliver anything over and above baseline work.

For the sake of perspective, consider the definition of each of these three vital traits:

1. **Attitude:** "A settled way of thinking or feeling about someone or something, typically one that is reflected in a person's behavior" (Google 2017).

   The odds of someone changing another's "settled way of thinking" are more than remote. The reality is that attitude is a choice. While you cannot control what happens to you, you can choose your response. And the quality of your career and life will depend greatly on the quality of that choice. Stoppable people choose the wrong response to setbacks, disappointments, rejection, defeat, or failure much—or most—of the time. Then, they wrongly blame someone or something for "giving" them a bad attitude.

> **Be thankful that no one or nothing has the power over your life to open your head, shove in a bad attitude, and leave you to suffer. *You* get to choose your thinking, your attitude, and how you will respond; and the game changer would not accept anything less.**

2. **Passion:** "A strong feeling of enthusiasm or excitement for something, or about doing something" (Merriam-Webster 2017).

   Feelings of enthusiasm and excitement caused by external stimulation are short-term spikes that fire you up for an instant and fade just as quickly. It is the excitement and enthusiasm birthed from within, from one's WHY, that burn consistently and intensely over time. No one can make you passionate about someone or something. Real passion comes from the heart out, not from the external in. Passion is not something you seize; it is something you are seized by.

> **"I have no special talent. I am only passionately curious."—Albert Einstein (2017)**

3. **Enthusiasm:** "Intense and eager enjoyment, interest, or approval" (Google 2017).

The word *enthusiasm* comes from the Greek word *enthousiasmos*, meaning that one is "possessed by a god, inspired" (Google 2017). To be enthusiastic, then, in essence means that you are filled with God.

While passion and enthusiasm are similar, the "eager enjoyment" aspect of enthusiasm makes it stand alone. This is the mindset to be content with and enjoy—to make the best of—any state you are in; to not only be enthusiastic when things go well, or when you have the wind at your back, but to enjoy the challenge of learning a lesson, leaving a comfort zone, making a change, taking a risk, and accepting coaching that hurts because you know it will make you better.

People with the right attitude, passion, and enthusiasm magnify whatever talent and skills they have exponentially. Those lacking any of these three qualities marginalize whatever talent and skills they have drastically.

Attitude, Passion, and Enthusiasm—Find a Way, Not an Excuse

LAPD's Cory Palka talks about the difference that "going A.P.E." made in setting three of his game changers apart from others:

Paul Jordan—Senior Lead Officer—LAPD Hollywood

"Are you one of those guys whose alarm goes off at 4:30 AM and you jump out of bed with excitement?" That is a question Senior Lead Officer Paul Jordan asked me recently.

Paul loves his job and his role as a community lead officer in an area that is some of the most well-known real estate in the country (Hollywood and Vine). Recently we had a paralysis with our homeless encampment cleanup efforts resulting from litigation, policy, and politics. The Department of Sanitation had gone totally absent in removing trash in and around homeless encampments.

We have various police units assigned to work on reducing homeless camps that dot Hollywood. My cops were pointing at other government agencies and new policy as excuses for why they were hands-off with enforcement and unable to clean up the camps. As a result, the homeless camps throughout Hollywood multiplied. Complaints poured in by community members, business owners, and politicians. But it was Paul Jordan who claimed this was more of an adopted police attitude of standing down and being passive, being focused on scapegoats rather than solutions. To spearhead a reversal of this attitude, Paul enthusiastically went to each roll call, met with unit leaders, and took to the streets himself to fix the problem. He reminded cops we can enforce crimes committed in camps; and, as a result, cop engagement intensified and arrests soared. Sanitation arrived after constant pressure, and the problem was fixed (for now). Paul never makes excuses, and works tirelessly. And when that is not enough, he works even more. He is an old-school, blue-collar cop. Right is right, and wrong is wrong. The only fuel he needs from me as his boss is my gratitude, my listening skills, and my physical presence occasionally at his community meetings or in the street. He is optimistic and fun, and sees the good in each day, but he is a passionate warrior of a cop.

Mike Ling—Lieutenant, Officer in Charge—LAPD Hollywood Entertainment District

Mike Ling is the lieutenant in charge of the LAPD Hollywood Entertainment District, and he oversees 80 cops and billions of dollars of Hollywood infrastructure. His team polices the Entertainment District . . . where over 11 million tourists visit annually, and where nightclubs and nightlife come alive. It's also prone to violent crime such as robbery, rape, murder, and aggravated assaults. Much of our violent crime in

Hollywood takes place in the District and is broadcast in local media and, at times, national media.

Mike has uniformed and undercover officers on his team. He effectively delegates my expectations to five supervisors. Mike has significant experience working with specialized units and has worked narcotics, gangs, and vice as a young officer.

Mike is a game changer because of his attitude, emotional intelligence, and win-at-all-costs attitude. He has the rare talent of seeing ahead and planning or front-loading to prevent issues from arising. He can relate to all cops, and obtains buy-in because he has empathy and compassion for them as individuals. He is known for his enthusiasm and passion in putting his guys first.

He studies my leadership style and knows the value of police partnerships in the community. I have spent hundreds of hours with developers, community groups, politicians, cops, and residential and business owners, and Mike knows the value of a handshake, eye contact, and conversation. Those relationships have created wonderful results, which lead to a better economy, more jobs, better schools, better lives, and reduced crime. Mike has seen crime collapse in the District since his arrival. He is personable, funny, and puts things into perspective. His energetic and positive presence ensures he is warmly received and highly respected by other cops and those in the community where he serves (Cory Palka, pers. comm.).

Palka sums up the essence of how game changers find a way—not an excuse—with his description of Hollywood Division Police Detective Doug Oldfield: "He comes to work to mix it up, get involved, engage, and produce. 'No' is never acceptable for Doug" (Cory Palka, pers. comm.).

This prompts a few questions: Do you have the attitude, passion, and enthusiasm to be a "Doug"? Do you have enough "Dougs" on your team? What *no*'s have you declared or accepted that could have been converted into results if you, or others, had gone A.P.E.?

> **"Catch on fire with enthusiasm and people will come from miles to watch you burn."**—John Wesley (Quoteland 2017)

Attitude, Passion, and Enthusiasm Are Separators and Accelerators

Brad Bartlett is president of Dole Packaged Foods in North America and Europe. He has been in the consumer products industry for four decades and has seen his share of undertakers, caretakers, playmakers, and game changers. He also makes a compelling case for the difference that attitude and enthusiasm make in helping to lift one to game changer status.

> Among equally talented people, what separates the solid performer from the "game changer" are two main things: attitude and enthusiasm. I would even suggest that, if these two traits were more visible in one person of lesser talent than another, the person with lesser talent likely would overachieve in a direct comparison. I first heard Lou Holtz speak at a trade function in the mid-1990s. He had already won the National Championship as the head football coach at Notre Dame in 1988 and was well on his way, compiling a resume to becoming a member of the College Football Hall of Fame—which did occur in 2008. He had great stories and a quick wit, but the three sentences that stuck with me that night were as follows:
>
> "Ability is what you are capable of doing."
> "Motivation determines what you do."
> "Attitude determines how well you do it."
>
> When you understand this and really think about what plays out in a business environment over a period of time, you see this as true over and over again. The person or group that has the attitude that there will be wins and losses along the way,

but that no matter what happens they will not come up short of their goal, are always the ones who seem to do much better than everyone else. Not only do their results tend to be better, but people like being around people who think and act like this. You naturally tend to gravitate to these kinds of people. You almost feel that some of it will rub off on you, so you want to be around that more than someone who has talent and knowledge but accepts what has happened in the past as a mandate for the future.

A major ingredient of having a great attitude is enthusiasm. I look at the two as being inseparable. How can someone have this powerful mental energy directed at goal achievement without having the fuel of enthusiasm to power the energy? I do not think that it is possible. When you view your best people over a long period of time, it is always the ones who display genuine energy, emotion, spirit, and passion for their individual or group results who not only are the best performers, but also tend to move upward more in a business environment. My background is sales. I remember very early in my career being in waiting rooms with 10 people sitting there with appointments ahead of me to see a buyer. I always thought that I only have one presentation to show, but this buyer is sitting through maybe 20 presentations today. What are they going to remember at the end of the day? You never really know, but I always thought what people would remember is the one person who came in with great energy and commitment for helping that buyer's business results. You may not have the right solution every time, but that buyer will remember you—and more likely than not call you back in at some point in time because you came in with a genuine desire to help a business situation and you showed great eagerness and intense interest to resolve the issue. If you have ever done a lot of interviews for job openings, who do you tend to gravitate toward when it is time to call back people for second interviews? Among relatively equal candidates, it is usually the ones who were the most enthusiastic about the opportunity that was in front of them.

One of my favorite stories that I tell about a person I have worked with for many years (whose picture would be next to the words *attitude* and *enthusiasm* if we had a company dictionary) is Bill Burokas. Bill has been a manager in our Northeastern area for almost three decades. He has been a consistent top performer every year regardless of the change in business environment and customer base. It does not matter what the challenges are; he is going to overachieve. What has always impressed me is Bill's desire to be the best that he can be and have his business unit achieve the highest results in the company. His attitude is a true example of setting out to achieve a goal; and nothing short of that goal would be satisfactory to him. He is his own judge, not the company or the supervisors. His standard is higher than anybody's, so if he hits his standard then it is the best it can be. You can always have a number of negative variables that impact a business year in and year out, but there are always opportunities—no matter how small they may be—that exist as well. When you discuss business with Bill, it completely revolves around the opportunities. It never dwells on the negative aspects. It is like saying that "there are always negatives. I know that they are there, but there is little or maybe nothing that I can do about those. I want to focus all my attention and energy against the factors that will have the best positive impact on my business. I only want energy spent on those. I do not want to talk about negative factors. It is a waste of my time." I could send him a note and describe all of the challenges facing his business unit for the upcoming year. He would immediately send me back the same number of factors that are working his way (or could work his way with some hard effort and maybe good fortune) that would attain his goals. This is a real mindset. This is the attitude of an overachiever. It is not contrived. It is real. He believes it's almost like athletes psyching themselves for a big game. You are in control of *you*, not always your environment.

One year for a sales and marketing meeting, I had the pleasure of bringing in Dr. Jack Llewellyn to speak to our group. Dr. Llewellyn is a world-renowned sports psychologist and corporate coach whose clients read like a who's who list of athletes in a wide range of different sports. He in turn has a similar list of corporate clients that fill up the Fortune 500 list, where he offers business guidance. When he spoke to us, he was working with this diverse group of people, but he was still on staff with the Atlanta Braves, who were about two-thirds of the way through the process of setting the current Major League Baseball record of 14 straight division titles, including winning the 1995 World Series. Jack asked me in advance of the meeting if I wanted him to score our group using his proprietary test that measured, among many things, one's attitude and enthusiasm for winning and losing. What sales manager worth anything is turning down that offer? I agreed to have him send it out to our people about a month prior to the meeting. It was a multiple-choice test, and Jack had said that you could not try to "game it"; and, after taking it myself, I found that was true. You were giving your feelings and opinions toward a series of statements. The choices, while different, were not completely opposite positions from one another as I remember it now. Everybody sent them in and, as you would imagine, there was great anticipation on the day of him presenting them to us during his talk. Each person would get his or her own results back in confidence, but Dr. Llewellyn would put up on the screen our overall company's scores and assessments of strengths and weakness areas versus other groups.

During the presentation, I was extremely happy to see that our group had scored very high versus the database that Dr. Llewellyn had from his years of testing other Fortune 500 companies. It made me feel good about our team, and reinforced some things that I already knew about them. Once everybody received his or her own confidential scores, you can imagine among competitive people that there was immediate bragging between parties about who scored much higher than the group, and some good-natured needling back and forth on who was holding the group back. As Jack went through the high and low scores by person and trait without naming names, he stopped in midsentence after talking about one of the low scores. He asked, "Where is Bill Burokas?" A couple of good-natured shots went out toward Bill from the audience, assuming that Bill was the one who may have done something that invoked this lower score for the group. Bill identified himself, and Jack found him in the audience. Jack then said, "If you were an 18-year-old baseball prospect, you would be the Atlanta Braves' first-round draft pick next year." It made the room go silent for a few seconds, and then cheers went out for that statement. That test told us what we all really knew, and it validated why this individual in our company consistently overachieves in a competitive setting. We knew it, and now a custom test by one of the most famous sports psychologists and corporate coaches in the country confirmed it (Brad Bartlett, pers. comm.).

Nothing causes you to stand out or move ahead faster quite like the right attitude, passion, and enthusiasm when applied daily, and regardless of external conditions.

Going A.P.E. Is About Selfless, Above-and-Beyond Contribution

Command Chief Master Sergeant Mike Klintworth is a military leader, and a creator of positive change in some of the toughest places on earth. He spent more than 27 years in the United States Air Force, where he served in a myriad of operational, management, and strategic-level positions. His experiences span positions from air traffic control operator to executive-level leadership in large, multi-national, and geographically separated military organizations of more than 3,000 personnel. Mike has deployed to Iraq, Afghanistan, and Croatia in support of Operations Iraqi Freedom, Enduring Freedom, and Joint Forge. From 2013 to 2014, Mike served as primary mentor and adviser to Afghanistan's most senior enlisted leader. While in that combat environment, he provided strategic guidance for structuring, developing, and leading a military force of 6,700 personnel. In Chief Master Sergeant Klintworth's world, the wrong attitude can create devastating conflicts and cost lives:

> After 27 years of military service, working as an air traffic controller, operating in a combat environment, and serving as a senior enlisted leader of large, multinational organizations, two qualities were consistent among military game changers.
>
> The first of those is *attitude*: a positive one. Game changers bring a positive attitude, which not only contributes to them approaching tasks, team projects, or change from a positive perspective, but it is also infectious—quickly spreading to teammates. I witnessed a great example of this during my one-year tour of combat duty in Afghanistan.
>
> Our 15-nation military team faced the unprecedented and admittedly daunting task of building an independent, self-sustaining air force for Afghanistan. Many of the challenges our team faced (cultural, monetary, and time constraints, and working in a very dangerous environment) were often navigated and overcome by game changers who approached the challenges with a "will do," positive attitude. Today, largely because of the attitude of these intrinsically motivated can-do warrior leaders, the Afghan Air Force is flourishing when years prior it was struggling for existence.
>
> The second quality a game changer exhibits is *passion*. Game changers have a passion for the mission, taking initiative, giving more than what's expected, and striving for excellence. They don't wait for their number to be called; they jump right in at the first sight of opportunity and often perform well beyond expectations.

The key to this quality is that game changers understand how what they do contributes to something much larger than their own self—the organization's mission success. I first realized this after asking a young military aircraft maintenance technician why they performed their duty with such diligence and passion. The response was: "If I don't perform my maintenance to the best of my ability, the aircraft could malfunction, causing the combat mission to abort or, worse yet, cost the pilot his life." Enough said.

As you can now see, it's attitude and passion that distinguish game changers from playmakers. And the beauty of these two qualities is that it doesn't take money to acquire them (Mike Klintworth, pers. comm.).

"Greater love has no one than this: to lay down one's life for one's friends."—John 15:13 (Biblica 2017)

Passion Brings Thirst for Improvement

Ed Bastian was part of the leadership team that helped Delta Air Lines navigate through and successfully emerge from the perils of bankruptcy, and then guide it to become an enterprise producing billions of dollars in profits annually. Now Delta's CEO, Bastian guides by example over 80,000 team members as they strive to operate at increasingly higher levels year after year. In Bastian's mind, the answer is clear when asked what key traits game changers consistently bring to the table that undertakers, caretakers, and playmakers lack:

I would say the clear delineation is passion. We have many bright, talented leaders at Delta. But those that rise above have a passion to pursue excellence in mastering their responsibilities. Their technical skills are outstanding, but that is not what separates them. They are in constant pursuit of enhanced performance, and their enthusiasm is infectious among their colleagues and customers. This is no longer a job to them; it's a part of who they are. And those who combine passion with a true heart of service are incredibly special. Their passion brings an entire organization to accomplish goals not thought possible (Ed Bastian, pers. comm.).

Sony Music's Troy Tomlinson affirms that elite performers have an ability to change and actually find energy within the change, saying, "They have a passion to share their art with the broadest audience possible, and have a deep, authentic, enthusiastic love and respect for their admirers and a like connection with their fans and teams" (Troy Tomlinson, pers. comm.).

UNSTOPPA
BULLET

The passionate cannot settle—they do not know how to settle—for the status quo. Their energy and excitement give them no choice but to change, improve, risk, stretch, and forge ahead despite the odds.

Going A.P.E. Helps You Thrive Under Pressure

Without question, anyone with a better attitude, more passion, and higher levels of enthusiasm is less likely to crumble when the pressure intensifies, and will demonstrate far greater resilience than the negative, lifeless, indifferent person. The passionate game changers' consistent ability to maintain the right outlook and think clearly helps them not only prevail through setbacks, but to learn more, become more, and contribute more as a result.

Coach Allistair McCaw puts it this way: "Game changers are better under pressure, as they see it as a privilege. They are able to step up and lead when needed. They embrace struggle and are solution finders, not problem seekers. They are also consistent in their behaviors, rather than moody or judgmental. They have an instinct and ability to make decisions better under pressure, accept change, and adapt to the unexpected better" (Allistair McCaw, pers. comm.).

Coach Samar Azem of Campbell University adds, "Resilience is another attribute separating the playmakers and game changers. Both individuals will be faced with challenges and likely have previously been faced with challenges. Children will not quit until they've failed at something a number of times. Once they become adults, unless they're resilient, they will settle for mediocrity, rather than push what the threshold past mediocrity will bring. Resilient individuals understand that failure is a part of that process and will therefore consistently put their fullest potential and controllable ability (work rate, energy, etc.) on the line, fearless of the implications of failure" (Samar Azem, pers. comm.).

Check Your Birth Certificate

When you check your birth certificate, I can promise you that you will not find "Has a great attitude, passion, and enthusiasm" listed anywhere on it. Nor will you find the words *negative, lifeless,* and *indifferent.* Nope, these are states you create for yourself, from within yourself, and based on how you choose to see life, the philosophy you create and embrace, and what you decide to make of your one opportunity on this planet. This is both great news and bad news. The great news is that living an unstoppable life anchored in the right attitude, passion, and enthusiasm are all within your control; no one can prevent you from becoming these things, or cause you to become unlike these things. The bad news is that if you have been accustomed to traversing through life as a sniveler, blaming other people or things for why you have the wrong attitude, or no passion and enthusiasm, then you are going to have to toss that crutch away and emotionally grow up so you can go up to your fullest potential as a human being. To summarize, the bad news is that *it is all on you.* The great news is that *it is all on you.* It all depends on how you choose to look at it. And someone aspiring to become unstoppable and live life dominated by the game changer mindset understands that choosing to see this reality as either great news or bad news is one of the easiest choices he or she will ever delight in making.

In summary, attitude, passion, and enthusiasm are inside jobs. They accelerate as you clearly define a compelling WHY, intentionally spend more time each day in your zone, and refine a more effective personal philosophy that shapes your mindset to think and act like a game changer—despite what's going on around you. Improving your attitude, passion, and enthusiasm starts with being fueled by a compelling purpose, owning it, taking complete responsibility for your current status in life, and doing all you can to engage in the thinking and actions that improve each and to discard or avoid the daily garbage that seeks to diminish them.

Mission Unstoppable

To become an unstoppable game changer, reflect and take steps on the following six points:

1. Knowing how much it will affect your attitude, passion, and enthusiasm, have you clearly defined your compelling WHY from Chapter 6? Is it in writing? Are you reviewing it each morning to help get focused and in the zone? If the answer to any of these questions is no, you should not go any further in this book until you take that action. The WHY fuels attitude, passion, and enthusiasm.

2. Knowing how much that staying in the zone affects your attitude, passion, and enthusiasm, have you clearly defined what you must do daily to spend more time in the zone, as well as which bait you must stop taking that pulls you out of it? What specific progress have you made?

3. As you review the definition of attitude ("A settled way of thinking or feeling about someone or something, typically one that is reflected in a person's behavior" [Google 2017]), what about your "settled way of thinking" must change for your attitude to improve? Might it involve blame, excuses, a focus on external conditions, the ease with which you are offended, your philosophy toward work ethic and doing all you can, or something else?

4. As you review the definition of passion ("A strong feeling of enthusiasm or excitement for something, or about doing something" [Merriam-Webster 2017]), what must you *start* doing (and *stop* doing) to increase your excitement and enthusiasm for what you do each day—despite external conditions that may seem to conspire against you?

5. As you review the definition of enthusiasm ("Intense and eager enjoyment, interest, or approval" [Google 2017]), where can you increase your sense of enjoyment when facing or enduring things like setbacks, rejection, a lost sale, or a bad game, by focusing on how you can become better and more unstoppable as a result of it?

6. Use additional and helpful resources to help yourself and others create game changer performance. Read John Maxwell's book, *The Difference Maker: Making Attitude Your Greatest Asset* (Maxwell 2006).

Going A.P.E. and living A.P.E. is a daily choice. Make it count.

CHAPTER 9

The Key to Mental Toughness

Faith is taking the first step even when you don't see the whole staircase.
—Martin Luther King Jr. (AZ Quotes 2017)

It would be difficult to find many people who would deny the role of mental toughness in becoming unstoppable in any field. Developing oneself to game changer status will require persistence, tenacity, focus, resilience, diligence, the right attitude, and faith. Speaking of faith, have you ever given thought to the direct correlation between faith and mental toughness? Frankly, how can one be mentally tough enough to fight and persist if one did not have faith that doing so would bring a worthy outcome or result? In fact, without faith in something positive or better, why even bother getting up at all each morning? It could also be argued that those who lose faith in tomorrow (or who do not believe the price they are paying or what they are enduring is worth the potential prize or payoff) simply quit—be it a job, a project, or a pursuit. Tragically, some decide to execute the ultimate "quit" and terminate their own existence when there is so little of an apparent promise in a better future. Without faith in *something*, what or who are you fighting for? Why get up so early, work so late, and go so hard from start to finish? Why bother to follow a process, or develop discipline, or forgo instant gratification unless you had faith it would benefit yourself or others, or would somehow help quench your WHY? The truth is you would not.

Based on the following definitions, consider this often-overlooked but undeniable connection between increasing faith and improving mental toughness, and begin to contemplate the fact that one of the best ways to increase your mental toughness is to intentionally do what is necessary to build your faith.

Wikipedia defines mental toughness as "a measure of individual resilience and confidence that may predict success in sport, education, and the workplace . . . frequently used colloquially to refer to any set of positive attributes that helps a person to cope with difficult situations" (Wikipedia contributors 2017).

Faith is defined as "complete trust or confidence in someone or something" (Google 2017). Think about it. If you did not have faith—that confidence in someone or something, be it yourself, your abilities, your future or destiny, the fact that hard work pays off or that the process works, or your family, coach, philosophy, religion, product, or team—would you have bothered to read this far in this book? Would you have even bought it to begin with? No way. You may not consider that your faith is very strong, or even adequate; but as you reflect on your life, would you have been likely to cope successfully with the struggles, setbacks, rejections, disappointments, or outright failures you have encountered time and time again and still come back to fight another day unless you had faith that something good was going to happen either that day or in the future? Again, no way! You probably have more faith than you realize. By the end of this chapter you will also have guidelines and inspiration to accelerate it, and become more mentally tough in the process.

"Optimism is the faith that leads to achievement. Nothing can be done without hope and confidence."—Helen Keller (AZ Quotes 2017)

Faith Is Personal

Where or how you build faith can vary depending on your values, beliefs, personal philosophy, religious affiliation, and more. For example, as a Christian, I will look to different sources to build and sustain my faith than the person of another religion, an atheist, or an agnostic would. I do not say this to diminish the methods others use to build their faith, but to explain what works for me. Actually, I would be remiss in writing a chapter on faith without having the credibility to explain where I derive my own. Even one who does not have a religious faith still has "trust or confidence in someone or something," or they would be void of passion, enthusiasm, goals, aspirations, or hope. Again, why would they even bother to engage in a new day unless he or she had a belief or expectation that something positive to their existence would occur?

Faith may come from numerous sources:

- Your own abilities or talents
- Your character
- Your experience
- Your knowledge or specialization
- Your teammates
- Your managers or coaches
- The strength of a product or service you sell
- The organization you represent
- A mission or purpose you are a part of
- A strategy you have devised to get where you want and what you want
- Your education
- Your resources
- Your reputation
- Your brand
- Your personal philosophy
- Your friends, network, or connections
- Your looks or physique

- Your God, or religious doctrine
- Your own willpower
- Your gender
- Your ethnic background
- And numerous other sources not listed

> "Believe in yourself! Have faith in your abilities. Without a humble but reasonable confidence in your own powers you cannot be successful or happy." —Norman Vincent Peale (b) (AZ Quotes 2017)

Your own faith most likely comes from a blend of many of the sources listed. Your challenge is to intentionally act and live in a manner that consistently builds and sustains faith (despite external conditions, obstacles, or setbacks) so that you continue to develop mental toughness and make progress on your journey to become unstoppable. Actions to this end can span topics covered in the past three chapters: defining a compelling WHY; being more aware of what it takes to put and keep you in your zone daily so you stay focused on performance; and leveraging the ensuing elevation in attitude, passion, and enthusiasm these actions bring.

But you should not stop there. I highly recommend that you also create some kind of structured routine—preferably in the morning— to intentionally clean up and focus your mind; to feed it a diet of faith-building words, thoughts, and philosophies, and offset the inevitable anxieties, fears, and despair your mind collects on a daily basis. Chapter 11, "Develop a Daily Mindset Discipline," will offer guidance in this regard, but this is a sensible place to plant that seed and encourage you to entertain the notion.

In my own case, my faith book (the Bible) tells me that I will gain faith by hearing God's word. So, as you might imagine, a portion of my morning mindset routine is reading through a series of devotionals, memorizing and reciting (hearing) specific passages, listening to inspirational material, and avoiding the toxic media and accompanying influences that would weaken my faith and nudge me out of my zone.

My intent in sharing this personal aspect of my daily routine is not to come off as preachy; so if you somehow choose to take offense and step out of your zone, that's on *you*! The fact is, I can only credibly communicate a process that works for me, and that happens to be it. I would expect you to do the same if you were writing this chapter.

Be Prepared to Fight for Faith

One key reason I am very disciplined in my morning daily mindset routine is that the Bible, which provides the basis for my philosophy for life, instructs me to fight for my faith. That is a bit of a wake-up call, because a warning to fight for something is an indication there will be attacks against it. These attacks often present themselves as persistent daily pressures from conditions, critics, doubters, setbacks, rejections, disappointments, and more that would hijack or deplete my faith if I am not continuing to strengthen it.

Without doing something, either knowingly or even unintentionally, to build or reinforce our faith, we will find ourselves with less of it. What you do is up to you, but that you do *something* proactive and intentional is not really optional if you want unstoppable game changer status to dominate your personal and professional life. You simply cannot develop the mental toughness necessary to become unstoppable without the faith that causes you to believe that you will be better, that things will be better, and that you will do better.

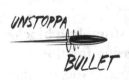

"The greatest legacy one can pass on to one's children and grandchildren is not money or other material things accumulated in one's life, but rather a legacy of character and faith."—Billy Graham (AZ Quotes 2017)

Faith Can Anchor Your Personal Philosophy

In Chapter 5 I presented Jim Rohn's insight on the importance of changing your philosophy in order to change your life. Without question, having a growing and strengthening faith as the bedrock of your philosophy will be a key ally in building your own unstoppable philosophy. When you have faith, you simply see people and things differently than those with little or no faith. Following are 11 examples, some of which you may wish to consider for inclusion into your own personal philosophy, as they can completely transform how you look at life.

1. **When you have faith, you do not care what the odds are, or who the opponent is; you expect to win.** You see a ranking or standing as something that is an explanation of what has already happened, not as a declaration of what is to be. You do not let the opinions of others define you, because when you have faith, you believe you will write your own script.

2. **When you have faith, you tune out the critic outside and mute the critic within.** You do not allow voices of others to define you, and you silence the doubtful murmurings from within by replacing them with words and thoughts of faith. You trust the process, your teammates, your instincts, your training, your philosophy, and the object of your faith (your God, yourself, or wherever your source lies).

3. **When you have faith, you are always looking for a way to win—a way around, a way under or over, or a way to break through.** You expect the best. You expect to win. But if the worst shows up, you believe you will prevail. You may not know how, and you do not have to know, but you still believe you will progress.

4. **When you have faith, you see potential stumbling blocks as stepping-stones, and setbacks as setups for the next step up.** You do not believe that things happen *to* you, but that they happen *for* you, and that you will find a way to use them and benefit from them.

5. **When you have faith, you do not believe you have failures, but that you have just received feedback.** You learn from it, become more as a result of it, and advance further because of it.

You do not frame disappointments as failure, but as a form of feedback you will grow and improve from.

6. **When you have faith, pain and pressure both focus and empower you.** You believe the ancient wisdom that declares that the olives pressed the hardest will produce the purest oil that burns the brightest. You use pain and pressure to rely more on your mental faculties, which increases focus, performance effectiveness, and results.

7. **When you have faith, you do *all you can* and then look around for others to lift.** You believe in the principle of sowing and reaping. And you also understand that doing less than you can makes you less than you are, so you always err on the side of going too far rather than failing to go far enough in both extending yourself and elevating others.

8. **When you have faith, darkness is temporary, defeat is imaginary, and breakthroughs are customary.** You understand that passing through valleys helps shape you, toughen you, and equip you for the journey to the mountaintop; that without the valley of tough times you would not have the toughness or endurance to make it to the mountaintop. Nor would you fully appreciate the view once you arrive there.

9. **When you have faith, the impossible becomes visible and the invisible becomes possible.** This is because faith is the assurance of things hoped for—a belief in what is yet unseen.

10. **When you have faith, you may fall down, but you are not defeated.** You may lose, but you do not quit. You may even lose your way, but you will not lose your will.

11. **When you have faith and things get tough, you do not wait your way out, wish your way out, whine your way out, or wait for someone to bail you out.** You get in your zone, put on your fighting shoes, and slug your way out. After all, faith is not a permission slip for passivity. Faith without action is just a disguise for wishful thinking.

"For we walk by faith, not by sight."—2 Corinthians 5:7 (Bible Gateway 2017)

Faith Under Fire

Tom Crean coached the storied Indiana Hoosiers men's basketball team for nine years, inheriting a program that had been on probation for three years and was at perhaps the lowest point in its 100-year-plus history. Not only did Crean save the program and turn it around, but he also led his teams to win two Big Ten Championships outright in his five final years at Indiana University, and three NCAA Sweet 16 appearances in the National Tournament. And every player who used his eligibility has graduated—*every player*.

In the 2015–2016 season, Crean's team won the Big Ten Championship outright and made a Sweet 16 appearance in the National Tournament, and Tom Crean was voted Big Ten Coach of the Year. The following season, after losing seven of his 15 players to graduation, the National Basketball Association (NBA) draft, and a season-ending injury (as well as suffering several key injuries to star players during the year), the Hoosiers still managed to be ranked as high nationally as number three, finish with a winning record, and beat two of the top-ranked teams in the country. However, at the end of the season the Indiana University athletic director abruptly fired Crean.

Interestingly, three months earlier Indiana University's head football coach had resigned under pressure from this same athletic director. There is a well-known axiom in organizations that when you have problems in an enterprise, you do not fix it at the bottom or in the middle; that a fish rots at the head—it starts to stink at the top first. In this case, the evidence would point to the athletic director. In organizations where weak leadership presides at the top, mental toughness among those working there is more essential than ever, so they stay focused on what they *can* control. You can also bet that any success within that organization comes in spite of the rotting fish, not because of it. The people surrounding him or her are to be highly acclaimed.

On five occasions between late 2015 and early 2017 I engaged at Indiana University in a series of sessions to train the players, staff, and members of the athletic department in mental toughness strategies and devising a personal unstoppable philosophy, as well as to teach culture and values. While dozens of personnel attended those sessions, I did not meet the athletic director, because he was absent from the meetings; thus I have no personal impressions to share. The comments, however, from beleaguered attendees that were shared with me after my sessions were unsettling, as they used adjectives relating to character and competence that I will not share here. There was consensus that he was unsupportive and did not have the backs of his people but was a puppet whose strings were pulled by wealthy donors and Varsity Club members. Accurate or not, this was the common perception shared by those working for him, and a prevailing culture of disgust and distrust was palpable.

Surprisingly, this same athletic director, who should be the most vocal champion of his staff, coaches, culture, and players, was negligently and noticeably silent when the notoriously fickle Indiana University fans booed their team at home games in Crean's final season. At that point, a strong and effective leader could have made a positive and unifying statement for the fans to stick together and rally behind the team as it fought through injuries and developed the new players. In fact, an action like this would have helped build morale and trust, and demonstrate support for the players, coaches, and staff. But by his silence, he implicitly invited more of the same. The players, coaches, and staff deserved better.

Perhaps you have found yourself, or find yourself, in a similar situation where you are oppressed by a rotting fish at the top of your department or organization. How do you keep your faith and stay focused when your boss, critics, constituents, and/or superiors are unsupportive, self-serving, or incompetent? When I discussed this with Crean, the classy coach refused any comment on the athletic director, other than to say he would never stop praying for him and his family. He did, however, share aspects of his sustaining faith and ensuing mental toughness in adversity that a reader may find helpful:

> The Bible says to train up a child in the way he should go and he won't depart. Growing up in church, the value of prayer, the church experience, and the lessons you hear get inside of you, and they got inside me. And this foundation makes it easy for you to go to prayer or read a devotional or Bible when life piles on. We're always just a conversation away from God and getting ourselves to a better place. The hardest thing is to eliminate the distractions around you. When you are truly talking to God, you are freed up to feel the calmness. It can be while walking, standing, kneeling in prayer . . . just those brief couple of seconds when you turn your mind over to God and talk to Him with something as simple as "Help me, Lord." When you do this, a calmness comes to you that builds confidence, energy, resilience, and faith. Faith focuses you on what's most important, which is what mental toughness is about anyway. Over the years, I've grown into not being affected by what people in the world think, or a fan might think, or a peer might think. When it really comes down to it, what's most important to me is "What does God say?" Asking this keeps you focused on what matters most, and in the zone (Tom Crean, pers. comm.).

You cannot change other people, but you can change how you respond to them, and decide to focus on what is most important despite their unhealthy influence.

Faith and Sacrifice

Think about this: Why do people change, risk, or sacrifice? In large part, it is because they have faith that the change, risk, or sacrifice will bring positive results. On the other hand, why *don't* people change, risk, or sacrifice? In part, this is due to a lack of faith that those actions will pay off, believing that the current course is the most productive route. They may have also developed a confidence—albeit a somewhat delusional one—that living in their comfort zone will get them all they want out of life.

Whatever changes you decide to make from reading this book will require faith, change, and some sort of sacrifice. Unless you believe the potential prize is worth the price, you will do nothing and remain the same.

Dan Barnette, based in Santa Monica, California, is one of the premier video editors in the movie industry. This specialized and high-stakes field of creating compelling trailers that make people say, "We've got to see that movie!" can make or break the momentum a new production needs in order to launch successfully.

Before editing trailers and commercials for movies and TV shows like *Gravity*, *Assassin's Creed*, *Stranger Things*, *Captain America: Winter Soldier*, and *Doctor Strange* (and winning numerous industry awards in the process), Barnette was a bartender in Columbus, Ohio, with a dream millions have shared—to move to Los Angeles and make it big in the movie business. What set him apart from so many is that he also had the drive and faith to put some shoe leather on those dreams, and make the sacrifices necessary to realize them. He worked in food service for nine years and sacrificed to save $3,000 to move to Los Angeles at 26 years old and chase his dream, giving himself five years to break into the film industry, whereupon he would return to his home in Ohio if unsuccessful. He explains:

I believe the traits that most separate *sometimes* performers from the elite in any field can be boiled down to three: drive, sacrifice, and appreciation. Personally, I have never been the most talented at any job I have ever had, but that has never held me back from being successful. I have always been willing to put in extra time and work to make up for what I lacked. My career goal was to be a film editor, and my first job in this industry was the most entry-level job available in the office: production assistant. I was ecstatic just to have my foot in the door. For the first year and a half I worked two jobs and seven days a week (my weekend job was a server) to be able to afford to live in Los Angeles. I was determined to take full advantage of this opportunity to achieve my goal. I started to stay after work to learn from the assistant editors. Eventually I began to show that I had developed new skills and was promoted to assistant editor, which allowed me to stop being a server. It took four years in total, but I was able to achieve my original career goal of becoming a video editor. A strong drive will help overcome any skill gap. No matter how talented, a lack of drive will ultimately leave those talents unfulfilled.

That leads directly into sacrifice. If you are not willing to make sacrifices to achieve your goals, then you will always come up short. My biggest sacrifice was moving from Ohio to California to pursue my dream of being a video editor. In college, I discovered a passion for film editing, and I quickly realized that if I wanted to follow that career path I would need to leave everything and everyone I loved in Ohio because the best opportunities are in Los Angeles. It seems so obvious to say it, but had I never packed my bags and left all that I knew behind, I never would have achieved one of my biggest dreams in life.

The sacrifices that I have made help me to appreciate the opportunities that I am given. I feel lucky that I am able to do what I do every day at work. It is a job that I enjoy, and I acknowledge the fact that many people cannot say that about their job. I try my hardest on every project that I am given the chance to work on. Whether it's a project I am excited by or not, I always put my full effort into the work and never phone it in. Every day is a chance to improve my abilities as an editor, so I don't want any one of those opportunities to go to waste, and I seize each one with the same intensity I did when I arrived at this company 11 years ago (Dan Barnette, pers. comm.).

"Whatever the dangers of the action we take, the dangers of inaction are far, far greater."—Tony Blair (AZ Quotes 2017)

For anyone still failing to appreciate the role that faith has in developing mental toughness (to create the willingness to change, risk, and sacrifice), consider the following insights from Doug Carter, senior vice president for EQUIP—a game-changing leadership training organization that has trained millions of leaders across every nation on Earth. After serving for 16 years as headmaster of a residential high school in Arizona for Native Americans, and nine years as president of a church-related college in Ohio, Doug became the vice president in charge of international operations for a nonprofit organization with approximately 300 employees on five continents. In 1996, after eight years of global travel to more than 30 nations, he accepted an invitation from noted author and leadership expert John C. Maxwell to help him launch EQUIP Leadership for the purpose of providing faith-based training, resources, and encouragement for leaders worldwide. Over the ensuing 21 years, Doug and EQUIP have served over six million leaders in 196 nations.

> It has been my joy to personally teach in 125 nations, but my focus has been on nations where men and women of faith daily face the reality of persecution and oppression. I have had the privilege of investing in and building deep friendships with Chinese, North Korean, Iranian, Middle Eastern, and North African leaders who have suffered under the hostility of tyrannical governments and the brutality of radical ideologies.
>
> An aging pastor in China and a young health care worker in Tunisia are examples of hundreds who have refused to abandon their faith or their divinely inspired dreams to serve others who struggle to survive in dark, difficult, and dangerous circumstances.

Between the ages of 20 and 63 this Chinese pastor was imprisoned seven times for a total of 27 years. His only crime was his Christian faith and his efforts to provide compassionate care for the poor and needy in village after village. During his 16 years out of prison he established thousands of churches that are offering holistic ministry to millions in China.

The Tunisian woman was beaten brutally and imprisoned in her own home for seven months, shackled to a post with ankle chains by her father and two brothers, who were enraged by her commitment to a faith they despised. After escaping imprisonment by her family, she committed her life to offering hope and care to other abused children and youths. Hundreds of young Tunisians are today living meaningful lives because of her investment in them.

Around the world, I have met hundreds of men and women who daily exhibit mental toughness. As I have observed them facing and overcoming unbelievable opposition as they faithfully serve others, I have concluded that mental toughness reaches a much higher level when coupled with faith.

Faith adds an almost unbelievable courage to mental toughness—a courage that will stand strong regardless of the personal cost.

Faith adds to mental toughness a depth of conviction that ignites a passion or fire that is unquenchable in the face of relentless opposition.

Faith adds to mental toughness a connection with a divine or supernatural Helper who inspires us to believe that all things are possible.

Faith adds to mental toughness a sense of compassionate purpose that transcends this life—a legacy of unselfishness that lives on in the lives of those we have influenced and in whom we have invested—a legacy of generosity that makes an eternal difference (Doug Carter, pers. comm.).

In summary, faith and mental toughness are indispensable to each other. Belief in better results, a better you, and a better world than you see currently is what fuels the mental tenacity to persist through difficulties, develop discipline, tune out critics, follow processes, and sacrifice what is necessary to become unstoppable in your chosen field. Everyone has faith in someone or something every day—faith that they will feed their bodies, love or be loved, find or live with purpose, be entertained, learn something, help someone, move one step closer to their dreams, and more.

But leaving the development of a faith mindset and its ensuing mental toughness up for grabs is reckless. You must be intentional in what you do, and in what you don't do, to build and strengthen faith. You must also be prepared to fight for faith, because the world with all its toxic influences, negativity, doubters, and valleys can drain and deplete a faith that is not reinforced. Actions like change, risk, and sacrifice are evidence of faith in something or someone with more promise than you are finding in your comfort zone, and will be essential in powering you to a point where game changer status dominates your life.

Faith forgets. Faith fades. Thus, faith must be reinforced to sustain and grow.

Don't Shipwreck Your Faith

A guilty conscience comes from cheating the process; failing to keep commitments; doing less than you can; being selfish, divisive, or corrupt; engaging in gossip or deceit; failing to prepare; and dozens of other acts (many of which are found in Chapter 7's list of zone busters). When you do something that violates your conscience, you are injuring your faith, because you know you have cheated or engaged in an activity that will eventually have consequences. And the fact that the consequences may not have materialized yet has you looking over your shoulder, living defensively—and without full faith—rather than moving ahead confidently in the direction of your dreams. Just as many of Chapter 7's list of zone busters will cause you to violate your conscience, the "in the zone" list of actions and mindsets will help you keep a clear conscience. On your path to become unstoppable it will be helpful to review Chapter 7 from time to time to audit your behaviors and make necessary adjustments. In fact, if you fail to reach a point where unstoppable game changer status dominates your life, it will not be because someone did you in, or because of bad luck. Most likely, it will be because you self-destructed, made poor decisions, repeated them over and over daily, and just could not manage to get out of your own way. *Do not* let that happen to you!

Mission Unstoppable

To become an unstoppable game changer, ponder and execute the following five points:

1. Determine what you should *start* doing daily to increase your faith. Can you include specific reading, listening, meditating, and the like in your daily mindset routine?

2. Determine what you should do *more* of to increase your faith. What current disciplines or habits that are productive can you intensify or spend more time with? If you currently have a morning mindset routine, is there something you could add to it? Is there something you could also do midday, or at the end of the day, to reinforce your faith with the right message?

3. Determine what you must completely *stop* doing or give up in order to increase your faith. Is there a destructive habit that hurts your confidence or shatters your conscience to the point your faith is diminished? Is there a habit you must renounce, or a person or group of people who do more to hurt your confidence, distract you, and influence you negatively whom you must stop spending time with altogether?

4. Determine what you should do *less* of that is currently building more fear and frustration than it is faith. Perhaps it is too much time spent watching reality television or doing mindless Web

surfing, or listening to and dwelling on negative news stories, political debates, social media wars, and the like—nonsensical matters that succeed only in taking you out of your zone and making you less effective.

5. Use additional and helpful resources to help yourself and others create game changer performance. For more on faith-based leadership, read my works on the subject, *How to Run Your Business by THE BOOK* and *How to Lead by THE BOOK*.

You cannot become unstoppable until you identify and give up what is necessary for you to go up: wrong thoughts, associations, habits, worries, doubts, and fears.

CHAPTER 10

Create Your Unstoppable Philosophy

Do not conform to the pattern of this world, but be transformed by the renewing of your mind.

—Romans 12:2 (Biblica 2017)

In Chapter 5 I introduced the concept of changing your life by changing your philosophy, and suggested that the decisions we make, the things we do or avoid, how we handle success or failure, how hard we work, how long we persist, and whether we change, risk, or sacrifice are all determined by our philosophy. Our philosophy is both a rudder that steers us through life and a filter that influences how we interpret and utilize what lies behind us, within us, and before us. It reflects our thinking and values, which determine our actions, in turn creating our results—for better or worse. As I suggested earlier, wherever you are in life now is overwhelmingly linked to your past philosophy.

For example, the list of "in the zone" actions or mindsets versus zone busters, as they were laid out in Chapter 7, really amounts to a philosophy on how to think and behave—a philosophy that in turn determines whether you spend your time in or out of your zone. This will then determine your level of focus on what matters most, which has incredible influence on the outcomes you create. Part of personal growth, and an essential strategy for becoming unstoppable, is to develop your personal unstoppable philosophy. Some of your philosophy may already be exactly what you need to become unstoppable. Other aspects may be holding you back, and they will need to be tweaked, totally revamped, or abandoned.

In this chapter I will share with you some key components of my own personal unstoppable philosophy—not because it is perfect, or even great (although it works great for me), but to stimulate your thinking about areas your philosophy should and could address. I review my philosophy daily (it is on my phone and computer) as part of my morning mindset routine. It is part of my daily discipline for "renewing my mind" so that I may be transformed into someone more productive, high-impact, peaceful, focused, and unstoppable.

It is not important whether you like, love, or hate my philosophy. That is not the point, and I am not putting it up for a vote. My purpose in presenting it is the same as my sharing in the last chapter how I build my faith. I can speak of matters like these credibly and with conviction since I endeavor daily to live my philosophy. I am not just writing about it or speaking to you theoretically. What you do to create, articulate, refine, or redefine your philosophy is completely up to you. Create a philosophy that works for you, just as I have forged one that works for me. My own has evolved a lot over the decades. There were thoughts and habits I had to renounce, and others that I had to adopt in order to help me get the results I desired. Your own philosophy development will likely follow a similar path.

Please note that my philosophy as stated does not define a level I live 100 percent of the time (I am a work in progress just like everyone else). But it is a standard I strive to, and I measure my growth by how well I live out its various aspects day in and day out. That, in itself, is a key benefit of actually articulating your personal unstoppable philosophy. By defining a standard, you will have something more specific to aspire to, increased clarity for handling various situations, and a benchmark for measuring progress and correcting deficiencies faster.

> "Change your thoughts and you change your world."
> —Norman Vincent Peale (a) (AZ Quotes 2017)

Excerpts from Dave Anderson's Personal Unstoppable Philosophy

All Things Benefit Me

My mindset is that everything that appears to happen *to* me actually happens *for* me, and is part of a vast cosmic conspiracy to help me become the best. I will find a way to use it to move me closer to my goals. Things do not happen to me; I happen to things.

I Stay Ready

I stay ready. I live my life on red alert. When the going gets tough I do not have to get ready, because I never got unready. I do not flinch. I expected it. I love tough times because they toughen me. I love tough times because they give me another test that I pass.

My Body Language Is Powerful and Empowering

My body language and energy level introduce me to others long before I say a word. I consider bad body language to be a bull's-eye on the back of losers who need to be rescued. Thus, I will be more aware of the impact that body language has on me, my teammates, and my foes.

I Renounce Excuses

I do not make excuses, because excuses weaken me and others. Excuses waste my energy and distract me from my WHY. I cannot have a killer instinct and make excuses simultaneously. Through excuses I become less of a person. Excuses also weaken the hearer, as they distract, diminish, and can cause compromise within another person. In this regard, excuses are selfish. Excuses are the DNA of underachievers. They are the language of losers. I renounce them.

I Own It

I take responsibility because owning my results empowers me and keeps me in my zone. Taking responsibility preserves my self-esteem, earns respect, and keeps me moving toward my WHY. Taking responsibility draws others to me, keeps me coachable, combats pride, and engenders humility. Taking responsibility intimidates the weak around me and empowers those aspiring to be strong. Blame makes me a victim. It is the anti-focus and is the language of losers. I renounce blame.

Haters Empower Me

I will not engage, combat, seek vengeance on, or give thought to constant critics or haters—those who see no *good*, but only *wrong* in what I do. I will surrender them to God and let Him deal with them. I pray that God builds within them the character traits they lack. I will use critics and their attacks to draw me closer to God in prayer, and conform more to the life of Christ. Their negativity weakens them, whereas my response to their actions keeps me in my zone and empowers me.

I'll Prove Myself

Yesterday ended last night. I will prove myself over again today. I will not borrow credibility, nor rehearse hurts from the past. I will make today a masterpiece.

I Don't Have Failures; I Get Feedback

I do not have failures; I only get feedback. Because of this, I feel no pressure when I make a mistake. I consider feedback a gift that energizes me and helps me grow. So where is the "failure" in that? There is none.

I Overlook "Offenses"

I do not give others the power to offend me. They can say and do terrible things, but they have no power over me, because I choose to invest my time, attention, and energy into what is possible and what is positive. An offense has power to weaken me only if I give time, attention, or energy to it. But I cannot give time, attention, or energy to offenses, because I do not acknowledge their existence in my life. And because they do not exist, they cannot hurt me.

I Cultivate Humility

God gives grace to the humble but opposes the proud. I will cultivate humility by serving others, admitting errors, taking responsibility, and striving to improve continually. I will subordinate my own comfort and welfare to what is best for my family, the team, and mankind. Pride comes naturally, but humility must be cultivated.

I'm the Competition

I do not compete with others because *I am* the competition. I hit my opponents hard, fast, first, and last, and I keep hitting them so they cannot get in a rhythm. Competing with others would indicate that I am trying to figure them out, counter their moves, or keep up with them. But my role is to set the pace, not to play catch-up. My goal is to dominate my opponents mentally, and make them figure me out, keep up with me, and counter my unstoppable approach to all I do. *I am the competition.*

I Don't Let the External Determine Outcomes

When things out of my control create obstacles, I still take responsibility and maintain control. If I blame conditions, it weakens me and I am admitting I do not have control or a solution. And I always proceed as though I have control and a solution, so I will take control and navigate through adverse conditions by focusing more intently on the things I can directly control. I will not let external conditions dictate the outcome. I own the outcome.

I Guard My Associations

I choose my associations carefully. I hang out with those who bring out the best in me, not the stress in me. No one I spend time with has a neutral impact on my life. In some way, they either elevate me or devastate me. While iron sharpens iron, acid corrodes it. I seek iron because I am iron. Some people I give up so I can go up. It does not mean they are bad people or even wrong; it means they are a bad fit in my life.

I Purvey Positivity and Possibility

I build and cleanse my mind daily, and throughout the day, with what is positive and possible. I give energy to what is good, pure, uplifting, virtuous, and within my control. When negativity and the world's darkness trespass on my mind, I recognize it and replace it with positive thoughts, gratitude, affirmations, and scriptures of light.

Pain Empowers Me

Living and working with pain makes me powerful, because I rely more on mindset—and mental is to physical what four is to one. Pain—physical or emotional—puts me in my zone. It sharpens my focus, stiffens my resolve, and baits my opponents. It causes opponents to dismiss me, which weakens them. Pain makes me dangerous to adversaries, because my survival instincts kick in and take me to a higher mental gear where I have nothing more to lose, and no longer fear pain, since I am already in pain.

I Have Situations, Not Problems

I do not have problems, only situations. Problems weaken; situations energize. Problems are negatives, and I will not automatically label something as a negative, because it may be a positive in disguise. I have problems only if I react wrongly to situations and thereby create problems.

I Use Pressure

Pressure does not exist on me, but *for* me. There is no pressure in the zone, because focus, energy, and confidence crowd it out. When I make a mistake, I keep pressure off by admitting it and taking it in stride. When I take responsibility, and focus on what I can control, I destroy pressure's chance of invading my zone. My unshakeable body language keeps pressure off me and puts it on others. When I decide to feel pressure, it is solely through my own choice, and results from deliberately enlarging my dreams to intensify my WHY.

I Beat Temptation

When unhealthy temptations present themselves, I do not flirt with them, and I do not fight them with my power; I resist them with scripture and by removing myself from unacceptable situations. Dabbling in sin breaks my attention, wastes my time, compromises my character, and weakens me. It takes me out of my zone. If I spar with temptation, I have given up focus and expended energy. If I resist with God's word, I keep my focus strong, my energy intact, and my mindset clear.

I Pursue Excellence

I aspire to be the best at what I do, but since I cannot ultimately control the capabilities of others, I will focus on being *my best*. True excellence is not being superior to another, for I may accomplish that and still be less than I once was. True excellence is being better than my former self. And I believe if I continually better who I am that I will ultimately become *the best*, period.

I Don't Do Revenge

I do not seek revenge, because investing my energy, focus, and time in unproductive pursuits weakens me. Revenge takes me out of my zone. Revenge brings me down to another's level. Revenge pridefully takes on a role reserved for God alone. I renounce revenge.

I Don't Fit In and That's Okay

To lead the orchestra, a conductor must turn away from the crowd. I do not try to fit in with the crowd, because the crowd is, for the most part, uninspired, unfulfilled, and average. It is never crowded at the top, but it is jam-packed at the bottom. There is intense competition among the mediocre. I work too hard to think, read, speak, look, or act like the masses. I set the pace and standard; I do not follow the pace and standard of others.

I Avoid Zone Busters

Zone busters take me out of my zone. They are fatal to focus, break momentum, distract me, and drain urgency and killer instinct. I avoid zone busters and if I slip into one I get out *fast*. Zone busters include bitterness, blame, excuses, revenge, gossip, disgust, judging, negativity, wrong associations, garbage media, sinful flirtations or activities, jealousy, envy, self-promotion, pride of any kind, selfishness, worry, self-pity, complacency, compromising with mediocrity, taking offense, and the like. Keeping my mindset right is my key to staying above zone busters and living at my potential.

They Don't Matter

People and things that are incidental do not matter in my life and can take me out of my zone if I give them attention. I master the art of not being offended or distracted by people and things that do not matter. This is because at the end of the day, as I pursue my dreams, most of the annoying people and nuisances I encounter daily are incidental, and will not ultimately matter unless I give them attention and foolishly invite them into my life.

I Make Things Right

If I have created a wrong, a misunderstanding, or the conditions for others to take offense—whether intentionally or not—I will take the first step to make it right. Reconciliation, accepting responsibility, and shunning excuses all keep me in my zone. Thus, by making things right, I stay powerful, focused, and in control. I am not responsible for how others respond to my reconciliation effort, and will not expend undue energy in the process. My responsibility is to reconcile quickly and sincerely, and take full responsibility—and then to not look back and to move on.

I Have No Bad Days

As I realize that many people will not ever *have* another day, I have decided that I do not have bad days. I may have less good moments, but never a bad day. It is only my wrong interpretation of a day's events that make it seem bad. Even days with extreme difficulty bring untold blessings and opportunities: to learn and grow, to become more, to set the right example, to improve my mindset, to make a positive impact, to lift others, to take responsibility, to rely more on God and watch for His hand in things, and more. I never complain about "long days" because I value life so immensely that I consider "long days" as bigger blessings—a chance to do more, become more, contribute more, and make a greater impact.

I Prioritize Relationships Over Rightness

Being right is less important to me than being in good relationships with others. I can work so hard to prove I am right that I take myself completely out of my zone. And I may be right, but I must weigh whether it is worth hurting a relationship over or getting out of my zone for. I am not a doormat, but I am wise to choose battles carefully. Expending energy to win every debate, prove every point, and set everyone straight will not help me become the best or lead me to my dreams.

I'm Grateful

I live with an attitude of gratitude. I begin my day rehearsing and recording what I am grateful for, not by inventorying my misery. I believe the more I am grateful for, the more I will have to be grateful for, because gratitude brings more blessings into my life, whereas ingratitude repels them. I also know it is impossible to be stressed out and grateful simultaneously. Thus, when I feel stressed I will pause to inventory my blessings, not what ails or irks me.

I'm "All In" Every Day

I go "all in" every day. I fully engage and give complete effort. If I do baseline work or demonstrate baseline energy or attitude, I can expect baseline results and a baseline life. Doing less than I can makes me less than I am. I answer the questions "How much is enough?" and "How much will you do?" with "*All I can!*" If it is not all I can, it is simply not enough.

I'm a Solution

My mind is wired for solutions. I will obsess over solutions, not situations. When a situation arises or something goes wrong, I do not look for scapegoats; I look for solutions and focus others on them as well. This keeps me and others in our zone. Even when I point out situations, I also suggest potential solutions. Staying solution-focused plays to win, keeps me in my zone, and avoids my falling into a reactive or victim status. I focus on solutions because I am a solution.

I Give Grace

Setting everyone straight over every little thing (especially things that in the big picture of pursuing my dreams do not matter) will take me out of my zone. I give grace, cut breaks, and forgive when others err. I believe grace and mercy are reciprocal, and as I give it, I will get more in return. Grace means unmerited favor—it is undeserved, but I give it anyway. I am gracious, not bitter; forgiving, not resentful; merciful, not vindictive. And this keeps me in my zone.

I Choose Cheer

Regardless of what happens to me, I choose cheer. I am in control of my attitude and emotions. My emotions do not control me. Choosing cheer keeps me in my zone, sets a positive example for others, plays to win, focuses on solutions, and lifts those around me. "I choose cheer" is my mantra, my reflexive response to apparent setbacks, disappointments, challenges, or situations I encounter. Since I believe everything that occurs happens *for* me and not *to* me, choosing cheer is easy for me.

I Am Light

Because I fill my mind with light, I bring the light of positivity, possibility, gratitude, and solutions into all environments and situations. My positive energy and attitude can shift a mood, a conversation, a crowd, or a culture toward what is good and possible. As I daily enlighten my mind, my mind activates fresh and uplifting words and actions. I bring light wherever I go because I am light wherever I go.

I Will Be Here and Be There

Wherever I am, my purpose is to *be there*. I will fully engage physically, mentally, and emotionally in the moment, the conversation, the activity, or the solitude. "Being here" will keep me in my zone. All I have guaranteed in my life is the present moment, so I will live in, relish, and maximize *that* moment. I will be neither in the past, which I cannot change, nor in the future, which I cannot control. I will *be here* and *be there*, wherever here and there may be.

I Don't Complain

Complaining takes me out of my zone. Complaining demonstrates ingratitude and entitlement, and likewise creates an unhealthy focus on negatives. Since I see myself as a solution, I do not have time to complain, as my focus is on creating answers or options—complaining would divert my focus from what is possible and positive. Since complaining often wastes precious time and energy on people or activities that do not matter, I stay above it and remain focused and moving forward. And because everything that appears to happen *to* me actually happens *for* me, there is nothing to complain about.

No Corrupt Words

I renounce corrupt words because they take me out of my zone, distract others, distort focus, divert attention from solutions, and contribute garbage to the atmosphere. Gossip, disparaging, whining, complaining, excuses, untruths, foolish speculations, deception, unfair criticism, and the like are corrupt, and I will replace them with what is edifying, graceful, merciful, possible, positive, moral, excellent, praiseworthy, admirable, and solution-focused. My words will lift and elevate, not level or devastate.

I Use the Power of NOW

There is power in NOW; there is not power in later, because I may not get a "later." Thus, I will act on what I know is right, possible, and positive NOW. NOW brings focus, energy, passion, and progress. NOW lets me learn, grow, and contribute. NOW is impactful. NOW is positive. NOW is possible. NOW is energizing. NOW is life, gives life, and helps me live life. I will do it NOW.

My WHY

I am laser-focused on a compelling WHY in my life. My WHY symbolizes my reasons and purpose—why I get up in the morning, and why anyone else should care. My WHY focuses me, energizes me, and gives me purpose, passion, and persistence. I review my WHY daily and it motivates me to act now, to prove myself over again today, to sacrifice, to pay the price, to make each day a masterpiece, and to be totally used up at day's end. I will not lose my way when I am focused on my WHY.

I'm a "Good" Finder

I condition my mind to look for what is good in any situation and any person, regardless of how dour, unproductive, or negative they may appear. When I am tempted to complain or criticize, I will instead find something positive to focus on, give energy to, and rally around. Finding good keeps me in my zone, positive, and focused on solutions and what is possible. I do not live in denial or deny reality. I simply choose to find good in what crosses my path, even when it seems bad, and even if what's good is only a glimmer. I am a "good" finder—a beacon of light in darkness, and a purveyor of possibilities amidst strife.

I Expect the Best

I go into every situation and begin every day expecting the best. I have prepared my mind to handle all situations productively, so of course I expect the best. Even if situations are less than the best, I intend to make them better. I also expect the best from others, and when I do not get it I don't react, but explain what the best should look like and focus on methods to make it happen. I expect the best, am prepared for the worst, and have equipped myself with the mindset and skills to transform the latter into the former.

Now Create Your Own!

Keep in mind that these thoughts and points do not constitute my complete personal unstoppable philosophy, but only what I am sharing in this chapter. These are thoughts I have learned and embraced from mentors, teachers, authors, books, sermons, and more, over many years. In addition to striving to live according to these points daily, I will continue to refine and redefine my personal philosophy in the future so that I may grow to new levels of personal and professional achievement, and expand my ability to help others do likewise. I share more in-depth applications of these particular points on my podcast, *The Game Changer Life*, which you can subscribe to at no cost. If you like any of these, you may wish to incorporate them into your own personal unstoppable philosophy. Tweak the words, adding or deleting parts to your liking. Whatever philosophy you create, refine, or redefine, it is important to review it often in order to rewire your mind in a manner that makes the thoughts and their subsequent behaviors reflexive, automatic, and natural.

"As a single footstep will not make a path on the earth, so a single thought will not make a pathway in the mind. To make a deep physical path, we walk again and again. To make a deep mental path, we must think over and over the kind of thoughts we wish to dominate our lives."—Henry David Thoreau (AZ Quotes 2017)

Mission Unstoppable

To become an unstoppable game changer, consider and act on the following elements:

1. Set aside time to write out your personal unstoppable philosophy. If you cannot articulate it, you cannot expect to execute it (at least not with consistency or conviction).
   - Understand that creating the ultimate unstoppable philosophy will be a work in progress, and something that you will continue to refine, expand, and redefine throughout your life.

- Ensure that your philosophy addresses key areas like handling success or supposed failure, work ethic, character choices, relationships with others, taking responsibility, and the like.

2. Determine which aspects of your current or past philosophy have caused you to do less than your best, settle for less than you should, develop unproductive habits, or make ineffective decisions. Ensure that these aspects of your philosophy are revised and improved.

3. Use additional and helpful resources to help yourself and others create game changer performance. Read the book *As a Man Thinketh* by James Allen (Allen 2015).

CHAPTER 11

Develop a Daily Mindset Discipline

I think how you start the day many times determines what kind of day you're going to have.

—Joel Osteen (AZ Quotes 2017)

If, after reading the past 10 chapters, you have identified either productive or destructive attitudes or habits in thinking and behaviors, the chances are good that these did not take root overnight. Rather, they were reinforced over time by certain influences in your life. For instance, the mindset to take responsibility may have started early on as parents or coaches stressed its importance over a matter of years. On the other (negative) side, you may have developed a go-to excuse that you have used for years or even decades. Perhaps it directs the blame to your parents, education, ethnicity, gender, and the like in order to explain away your lack of results in a certain area, or to justify poor character choices with the belief that "This is just the way I am." If the latter mindsets and habits have gradually become ingrained into your being over time, you might also expect that undoing them or replacing them with healthier mindsets and habits will not happen overnight, but will require a process—over time—to become part of your more robust, unstoppable philosophy.

You Cannot Simply "Not Have" a Mindset

Mindset is defined as "the established attitudes held by someone" (Google 2017). The question is not whether you *have* established attitudes, but rather what those established attitudes are.

This prompts additional questions, such as: What impact are your established attitudes having on your life, and how can you improve those established attitudes? Your mindset will be shaped in large part by the beliefs you embrace, as well as the people and activities you spend most of your time with. This is why an intentional and structured mindset routine is so important. Becoming unstoppable so highly depends on your developing the right established attitudes that you cannot leave it to chance, or leave your mindset up for grabs. Frankly, you can either deliberately shape your mindset with the right philosophies and attitudes or let your mindset be shaped for you by media, social trends, popular thinking, fads, and fleeting philosophies.

Our mindset and character will develop in due proportion to those aspects that we give our time to exercise and develop.

You Cannot Microwave Mindset

If you wanted to lose 20 pounds or get in better shape, you would need to follow a process, develop a new discipline, and stay consistent over time. You couldn't just declare that you want a better body, do 10 sit-ups, and then expect to wake up with six-pack abs. We understand this principle of process as it relates to the body, but then we wrongly believe that we can somehow microwave our mindset into unstoppable game changer status with the mental version of doing 10 sit-ups. We think that by reading one book, getting a pep talk, attending a seminar, or listening to an inspirational speaker, without any subsequent follow-up to close the gap between knowing and doing, that we have "renewed our mind" and have now been officially transformed. Rather, we should understand that, as with anything excellent and worthwhile, we must forgo the microwave approach and "crock-pot" it. We must follow an effective and structured process, *over time*.

 **Human beings develop to their potential in a structured environment, following a consistent process over time—not by dabbling in a new discipline, then a new fad, and then another whim.**

The Pain, Power, and Pleasure of Process

Process facilitates focus, discipline, and consistency. No one has to love, or even like, a process; you have just got to get motivated about what the process will do for you and follow it every time, over time. Frankly, I find the process for losing a few pounds bothersome. I stop eating foods I enjoy, start eating foods I do not like, drink light beer, and—perhaps worst of all—subject my body to cardio workouts, rather than more enjoyable tasks like lifting weights. But what I find, and loathe to admit, is that once I begin to see results of consistently following the process, I no longer feel that I am *paying* a price, but am actually *enjoying* the price. I still detest parts of the process, but the rewards offset the rigors. The process evolves from being *painful* to *powerful*, as it creates pleasurable results.

Developing a mindset discipline—a daily discipline—may also have components in the process you find bothersome. You may have to get up earlier to read or listen to inspirational material, watch less trash television, and read fewer tabloids. It might mean you reduce your involvement from three fantasy football leagues to just one, and forgo stupid and unwinnable political or sport team debates on social media with trolls who thrive on getting under your skin and into your head. But the payoff of a renewed mind and a transformed, unstoppable life will dwarf the pain of adjustments you make along the way. Again, the "pain" of process becomes powerful as it creates pleasurable results.

> "Everybody wants to go to heaven, but nobody wants to die."—Joe Louis (AZ Quotes 2017)

What You Do Is Up to You

Just as there is not a one-size-fits-all WHY, or personal philosophy, there is not a single recipe for an effective mindset-building routine. What you do is up to you; that you do *something*, and do it *consistently*, is not optional if you want to develop a mindset that accelerates your journey to become unstoppable. While many successful people have intuitively developed some sort of daily discipline to improve their minds or attitudes, the more structured and intense your mindset building routine is, the more effective it will be overall. Here are three suggested guidelines:

1. It is best to engage in a mindset routine in the early morning, when there are fewer demands on your time or potential interruptions. This also helps set the tone of the day and puts you in your zone before you are in the trenches.

You never have to recover from a great start.

2. It is helpful to do something to maintain your mindset as the day wears on. Just as you cannot eat healthily for breakfast and then pig out on honey buns and moon pies the rest of the day and expect to get your body in shape, you cannot expect a dose of morning inspiration will withstand an onslaught of negativity, media trash, unproductive associations, and faulty philosophy throughout the rest of the day.

3. Just as you tweak and enhance a workout routine occasionally to keep it interesting and stretch your abilities, so must you do with your mindset routine.

A Sample Routine

My own mindset routine started by accident three decades ago. In fact, I did not even realize I was developing a routine, but simply wanted to do something to improve my attitude to help me perform better at work. I had just started a new job selling cars, and made the mistake of trying to fit in with the other salesmen. As the new guy, I thought fitting in was important; but it did not take me long to realize that the people I was spending time with and emulating were unsuccessful at their work, and mostly miserable in life. They were lazy and chronic complainers who had a know-it-all attitude—and their anemic results reflected these traits. Before I went to work each day I started reading one chapter from the Book of Proverbs. Proverbs has widely applicable wisdom that transfers very well into the sales field, and since there are 31 chapters in the book, I made it a practice to read through the book once a month—a discipline I continued for many years. While I could not credit my new routine entirely, it was a major factor in my becoming the top salesperson for 15 consecutive months before taking a job in management—a fairly fast track for a new salesperson in the automotive retail business.

Over the years, I have continued to add elements to enhance and supplement my mindset routine, and three decades later I cannot fathom beginning a day without first getting my mind cleaned up and focused, and planting myself firmly in the zone by following my routine. To give you an idea of what you can include in a mindset routine, I am sharing key elements of my personal regimen here. Keep in mind that my routine began three decades ago with reading a few paragraphs in Proverbs, and evolved into this over time. I am not suggesting you do this, or that it is for everyone. I am instead supplying another example I can speak of credibly since it is real in my life and has produced consistently solid results.

- I fill out a gratitude journal, which provides entries to include what went *right* the day before—a key difference from how many people begin their day, which is to inventory the prior day's misery. I have used *The Simple Abundance Journal of Gratitude* by Sarah Ban

Breathnach (1996) for 20 years. By beginning my day with gratitude, I shift my attitude to a far more productive state.

- I review my WHY. I have it on my computer as well as on my phone, so I can also review it during downtime at airports, on flights, and the like. I have my WHY summarized in two sentences, and then broken down into numerous specific components and categories.

- I read through a series of daily devotionals that I subscribe to by e-mail. There are seven in all: one from Joel Osteen, one from Dr. James Kennedy, a Proverb of the Day, one from Wisdom Hunters, two from the Institute in Basic Life Principles' Daily Success program, and a Marketplace Leaders devotional, *TGIF*, by Os Hillman.

- I pray.

- I review a series of affirmations that summarize the philosophy points I shared in Chapter 10.

- I listen to a five- to six-minute motivational piece on a USB flash drive. There is one clip for each day of the month. After the month is over, I listen to it again the next month.

- I recite and memorize key scriptures that address aspects of life and faith.

- I review daily priorities.

The routine to reset my mindset takes between an hour and an hour and a half, depending on the depth and breadth of the devotionals, and how much follow-up research I do as a result of the devotionals to learn more on a particular topic. But I can say this with conviction: By the time I walk out the door in the morning, while I may not be the smartest or most educated guy in the arena that day, no one will outwork me, outfocus me, outfight me, or outlast me. I am so focused and energized that I am ready to charge hell with a squirt gun.

"The secret of your success is found in your daily routine."—John C. Maxwell (AZ Quotes 2017)

Start with Five Minutes

If you have no structured or consistent mindset routine at all right now, could you find just five minutes to start with? Could you maybe rise earlier and skip the newspaper, social media, or morning talk show to renew your mind with thoughts and philosophies that can change your life, help you impact others, and become unstoppable in the process? If you already have a routine, is there a way you can enhance it, reenergize it, or stretch yourself with something new? One key reason why I launched my podcast, *The Game Changer Life*, is to provide people with something motivational, inspirational, and educational to listen to before they leave home or during their drive time.

Here is another thought: Sometimes just giving up certain habits and tendencies does wonders for building your mindset. Spending less time with unproductive tasks, people, or other influences goes a long way in delousing your mind from the garbage it tends to pick up as you go through an average day.

If you have become successful without an intentional daily mindset routine, consider how unstoppable you will become once you're deliberately shaping your mind daily with what is more positive, possible, and productive.

Meyers Leonard makes millions per year as a National Basketball Association (NBA) player, and was introduced to the concept of a regimented mindset routine during a seminar at our LearnToLead Elite Center near Los Angeles. Despite his success on and off the court, there is no way he is leaving his mindset up for grabs:

As an NBA player I not only have to continually work on my skills and physical strength but, more importantly, I have to work on my mindset. As Bob Knight once said, "Mental is to physical as four is to one." I couldn't agree more with that statement. Daily, I go through my mindset routine, which includes positive affirmations, scripture, and core values, among other things. This season, my mindset routine has allowed me to stay positive and focused even when things have gotten difficult. In the past, I would have been much more frustrated and down on myself. My mindset routine has been key for me in my life as a professional basketball player, and also in my everyday life (Meyers Leonard, pers. comm.).

EasyCare's CEO, Larry Dorfman, shares:

My morning mindset routine has truly changed the game for me. Rather than jumping into the fray, checking e-mails and social media, texts and phone messages, I spend half an hour to an hour doing five things: meditation, learning something new, writing in a gratitude journal, reviewing a list of affirmations, and listing the three to five things that *will get done that day*.

I do allow myself to vary the order of these based on what moves me upon waking, but all are done before I do any work, e-mail, etc. Meditation is normally first, as it really sets the space up for me. Just 12 to 15 minutes puts me in a calm place to move into the other.

Affirmations are really cool. I believe mindset is just an established set of attitudes and desired behaviors we hold and believe in. Unconscious understanding of them is the key, and the only way we get to that is by repetitive study of what we have determined to be our affirmations. It is just like anything else we want to master; it takes thousands of hours (Larry Dorfman, pers. comm.).

> **"The more man meditates upon good thoughts, the better will be his world and the world at large."** —Confucius (AZ Quotes 2017)

You may be concerned that over time a daily mindset routine could become redundant and lose some of its impact. This is why it is important to blend revisiting and perfecting core principles, as you build your routine with new and fresh components over time. You may also want to consider what Dave Wilson of the Preston Automotive Group says on the matter:

> I have always believed in personal growth, but I never was actually committed. About 10 years ago I met Dave Anderson. We brought Dave in for leadership training. I noticed every time Dave was consistent, and some would say redundant. Some of my leaders didn't like his redundancy. For me I thought it was awesome. I started saying the phrase "Redundancy Rules." Dave has an amazing way of tying lessons from previous seminars into what he is saying and blending them with new lessons for continued growth. There is a connectedness that allows transfer of learning from seminar to seminar, building a strong progression over time.
>
> Since meeting Dave, my personal growth plan is on steroids. I read leadership books daily. I share these books with my leaders and we discuss them weekly. It's amazing how training daily has changed our culture and ultimately our lives (Dave Wilson, pers. comm.).

Great mindsets and unstoppable game changers are developed daily—not in a day. Until you're perfect, it's not redundant.

Right Mindset Helps You Max Out the Moment

We live in a world obsessed with outcomes, and, while we are all eventually judged on the outcomes we produce, we will create greater outcomes if we condition our mindset to max out the moment and focus on the activities that are more likely to create the right outcome (primarily the things we can control). And you are more likely to be thinking in those terms after some proactive morning mindset work.

Sony Music's Troy Tomlinson explains this dynamic in relation to songwriting: "You have to find a way to immerse in the moment and divorce yourself from the results. If all artists are thinking about is making a number-one record, or a song of the year, they won't have a great day in the studio that day. That doesn't mean you shouldn't have goals; but, when in the midst of battle, elite performers focus their minds and energies on what they can control" (Troy Tomlinson, pers. comm.).

You are not likely to be disposed to focus on what you can control when your undisciplined mind is obsessed with what it can't control: critics, the jerk in traffic, horrific news stories, what the president said, the stock market, and the like.

Fight Like Ferrell

I first met Yogi Ferrell when I spoke to the Indiana University men's basketball team in their film room on December 5, 2015, after a big loss to Duke. The Hoosiers were 5–3, and the restless Bloomington unfaithful were already up in arms. Ferrell sat in the front row during my presentation on "How to Stay Hungry with a Red Belt Mindset," and here is what I remember most about him: The guy did not blink for 45 minutes! He was locked in like a laser. I soon learned that was how six-foot point guard Yogi Ferrell approached pretty much everything: tireless work ethic, unstoppable spirit, complete dedication, and a relentless mindset filled with focus and fight. He was in his senior year, was the team's leader, and left that meeting to lead the team to 12 consecutive wins, an outright Big Ten Conference championship, and a Sweet 16 appearance in the National Tournament. Oh, and in the process, he became the all-time assist leader in Indiana Hoosier history. Unlike the occasional playmaker, Ferrell's consistent mental approach, work ethic, and results made him a game changer.

After the season ended, and to prepare for the upcoming June 25 NBA draft, Ferrell went on a whistle-stop tour across the country, working out for 16 NBA teams (over half the teams in the NBA). He did so with a chip on his shoulder—despite his accomplishments, he was not invited to the NBA combine to showcase his talents. In fact, he turned the letter of rejection stating, "You have not been invited to the NBA combine," into an image for his phone's background screen. This became part of his WHY, a central aspect of his daily motivation.

In an interview on his path to the NBA, Ferrell told me he thought 11 of the 16 workouts were worthy of impressing the team's general managers with his ability to play professionally, and his hopes for earning a shot on an NBA team were high. On draft day, Ferrell hosted a celebratory draft party with family and friends, anxiously awaiting the big moment when his name would be called as an NBA draft pick—only it did not come. No one wanted the all-time assist leader in Indiana history, a member of two conference championship teams, one of 10 finalists for the Bob Cousy point guard of the year award, and one of just 35 men on a midseason watch list for the coveted Naismith Trophy. Ferrell did not consider this as failure, but as feedback. And he got to work. The next few months looked like this:

- He joined the Brooklyn Nets for the NBA summer league, but was waived after three preseason games.
- After a brief stint with the NBA Development League (D-League) Long Island Nets, Ferrell was reacquired by Brooklyn, played for three weeks, and was then waived again.
- After being waived the second time by the Nets, Ferrell changed his phone's background screen to say, "Don't complain, just work harder." He didn't have a victim's mindset. He didn't make excuses. He didn't blame anyone else. He owned it and kept working harder than ever, being a game changer all the way.
- Two days later, on December 10, Ferrell was reacquired by the Long Island Nets. Ferrell's terrific coach there, Ronald Nored, told him that if he wanted to make it to the NBA, he had to *want* to be in the Development League—to max out the moment. That was easier said than done since the food, equipment, accommodations, venues—everything about the D-League—were a step down from

the NBA. But Ferrell took the message to heart and shifted his mindset to max out each moment and fight his way into the NBA.

- Amidst these transitions, Ferrell and one other player were given a tryout with the Philadelphia 76ers, who subsequently chose the other player over Ferrell (this other player was later waived).

- On January 28, Ferrell's hard work paid off when he earned a 10-day contract with the Dallas Mavericks. He had 10 days to prove himself. So strong was his mindset and resolve that he told friends and family the day he signed the 10-day contract, "I'm staying here."

- Ferrell amazed the staff with how quickly he memorized the playbook, and was put into a starting position during his first game with Dallas against the formidable San Antonio Spurs. Ferrell went into the game with an aggressive rather than starstruck mindset, knowing that even stars like Tony Parker and Kawhi Leonard had weaknesses. He was determined not to be awed by them or respect them on the court as he normally would off the court. In 36 minutes Ferrell scored nine points and seven assists in a 105–101 win. The next day he scored 19 points in a 104–97 win over the champion Cleveland Cavaliers. He then put in 11 points with five assists in a win over the 76ers, and made national sports headlines with 32 points in a 108–104 win over the Portland Trail Blazers—becoming just the third undrafted rookie in NBA history to score 30 points or more within his first 15 games. This particular game with Portland came on the final day of his 10-day contract. When the plane landed in Dallas from Portland, Ferrell was not allowed to exit until he had signed his new two-year deal with the Dallas Mavericks! At roughly 2:00 AM, Ferrell was the last man off the plane, and was a victor in his quest to fight his way into the NBA. He possessed the right skills and talent for sure, but it was all powered by a mindset to not let up, not look back, and not give up.

When I asked Ferrell what his mindset was now that he had an NBA contract, he replied, "I was told it was easy to get into the league, but that it's hard to stay. Now I'm focused on this: How can I find different ways to stay in the NBA? How can I make mind and body stronger going forward for many years to come? How can I continue to play so well that they can't deny me, that they will keep me for my ability as well as for my character?" (Yogi Ferrell, pers. comm.).

Throughout his fight to earn a spot in the NBA, Ferrell focused on what he could control, stayed in his zone, was powered by his WHY, and developed a mindset to max out the moment. This mindset had been developed over time, not overnight. And at the right moment, it made him unstoppable. Like so many unstoppable performers in various fields, Yogi Ferrell is not an overnight success, but an over time success. In his youth, he "was ranked the number one player in his class as a fifth grader by Clark Francis in the controversial 'Hoop Scoop' rankings in 2004," and being "just 10 years old and 4′10″, Ferrell already had a crossover dribble, could hit a running jumper in the lane, and make one-handed bounce passes that hit teammates in stride" (Wikipedia 2017). As the years passed, his talent developed, his skills were sharpened, and his mindset was strengthened. When his time came, he was ready. This prompts the question: When your next breakthrough opportunity comes, will you be ready? You cannot wait until then to prepare, or you will miss it. And if it does not come easy, are you prepared to fight like Ferrell? Preparation all starts with your mental game, an aspect of your success that will be greatly accelerated by your own version of, and commitment to, a daily mindset routine.

Act like a challenger even if you are a champ. Challengers are hungry and humble, and have something to prove. Champs can become cocky and complacent, and can turn into know-it-alls.

Mission Unstoppable

To become an unstoppable game changer, act on and employ the following four points:

1. Commit to a consistent, structured mindset discipline (a routine that can accelerate your growth so that unstoppable game changer

status dominates all aspects of your life). Consider these elements of your mindset routine:

- Start early in the day and maintain your mindset discipline during the day. Bring closure in the evening with something to clean your mind up before you sleep.
- Read e-mail devotionals.
- Keep a gratitude journal.
- Review your WHY or other goals.
- Listen or watch inspirational podcasts, videos, and audio material.
- Create affirmations that will rewire your mind. You can use aspects of your personal philosophy as components.
- Listen to *The Game Changer Life* podcast for additional messages to reinforce the material in this book.
- Meditation, prayer, positive music, and the like are also powerful aspects of an effective mindset routine.
- Memorize scriptures or passages that reflect your religious beliefs.
- Review key daily "must get done" items.
- Do it *every day*. And EDMED! (Every day means every day!)
- Make a more conscious effort regarding what to avoid during the day—zone busters in particular—that have the potential to reset your mindset with garbage.

2. Embrace the mindset process and understand that you can transform yourself by renewing your mind, but it *will* take time. Remember the words of Dave Wilson: "Redundancy Rules."

3. Learn to fight like Ferrell. When things get tougher, you get tougher. When they get harder, you work harder. But realize that it is essential for you to be mentally prepared for the opportunity or setback *before* it happens, and your mindset routine will help get you there.

4. Use additional and helpful resources to help yourself and others create game changer performance. Watch my free "Business Facts of Life" video series, available in the "Free Resources"

section at www.LearnToLead.com. They apply to all organizations, not just businesses, and they help in building the right mindset.

"I fear not the man who has practiced 10,000 kicks once, but I fear the man who has practiced one kick 10,000 times."—Bruce Lee (AZ Quotes 2017)

CHAPTER 12

The Unfathomable Power of Example

Example is not the main thing in influencing others. It is the only thing.
—Albert Schweitzer (AZ Quotes 2017)

Example Is a *Very* Big Deal

I am convinced that most people have no idea of how powerful their example is to others—not just in what they say or do, but also by what they *don't* say or *don't* do. The power of your example is unfathomable. The sooner you understand that, the sooner you will start holding yourself to a higher standard of thinking and behaving that is in alignment with living at unstoppable game changer status.

Grace Made Man

In the same December 5, 2015, meeting with the Hoosiers where I first met the unblinking Yogi Ferrell sat his friend, roommate, and teammate Troy Williams, a then junior with National Basketball

Association (NBA) aspirations and abilities. Williams's experience is another incredible story of an undrafted player who fought his way to an NBA roster spot with the Houston Rockets. In my talk to the team that day, I mentioned how at their age I was living in a furniture-less house with rats, and shared principles for working one's way out of tough spots. I talked about the contrast between then and now, and how after my life started to gain positive financial traction, all my WHY goals prioritized the material; but then I explained how that evolved to a more external WHY that included the starting of a nonprofit foundation that helps feed more than 400 orphans daily. I mentioned that, over time, I had achieved all my "B" goals, but that I never liked when people referred to me as a "self-made" man; instead, I considered myself to be a grace-made man. I believe it was through the grace of God that I moved out of the muck of financial misery and into the blessed life of being able to help others.

Later that afternoon, while I was watching the team practice, Williams ran up to where I stood, stopped, and said, "I really like what you said about being a grace-made man," then continued with his drills. I did not know just how much he liked it at the time, but a short while afterward I knew exactly how much when I received a text from him with a photo of his new tattoo that said, "Grace Made Man." He wrote, "I told you I liked what you said that day."

We can never underestimate the ability we have to influence others through our words or our example—either to impact them for good or to influence them to their detriment. We should take seriously that our example for good, or for evil, may one day become a tattoo that another wears on his or her mind or body for the rest of his or her life.

UNSTOPPA BULLET

When your thinking and behaviors change and you begin to move toward game changer status, it's likely your greatest payoff will not be what you become or get for yourself. Perhaps instead it will be the example you inspire others with that can change their lives' aspiration and trajectory.

Think about that last statement. How many kids has Michael Jordan inspired to work harder, practice more, and improve because of his example? The answer is incalculable. And while you may not ever impact others at his level, your new philosophy, mindset, discipline, attitude, passion, enthusiasm, and consistency can (and will) inspire those closest to you, those who work with you, those for whom you work and whom you serve, and even the incidental contacts you have met but once and never cross paths again.

Everyone Leads by Example

For 20 years, people attending my seminars have told me, "I want to learn to lead by example." My reply is that they already are, that everyone leads by example. That is not in question. The question is: What is the example you are leading or living by? If you lie, cheat, steal, blame, take shortcuts, and gossip, you are leading by example—a dreadful example! If you own it, renounce excuses, outwork everyone on your team, and then look for ways to lift others, you are also living by example—an example that can change someone's thinking and life. In reality, undertakers, caretakers, playmakers, and game changers all lead and live by example, but the difference in example is like comparing prisons to penthouses.

How much would a game film of your typical day sell for if marketed as an instructional video for how to become an unstoppable game changer? If you are not living it, how will you inspire it in others?

There Is No Sole Game Changer Mold

There is not just a single way that you can influence others with your example. In fact, you may not even realize you are impacting others while it is happening. But when you shift your mind and life into a higher gear and begin to pull away from the pack, you can be assured that more eyes will be on you, and what you do or say has the potential to elevate or devastate (to be magnified much for good or for bad). The ancient wisdom is true: To whom much is given, of him shall much be required. And I would add to that: "So don't screw it up!"

Arlington Independent School District's director of athletics, Kevin Ozee, recalls two game changers who positively influenced others in different ways:

> A game changer that comes to mind for me is Coach Hal Mumme. Coach Mumme was made fun of and bounced around from job to job, but he was able to take a few offensive football concepts that had been around since the 1950s and tweak them to his players' strengths. Now, almost every college and high school program in the nation runs some form of Coach Mumme's Air Raid Offense. The number of head coaches that have been spawned from Coach Mumme's staffs is mind-boggling as well. Who would have ever thought that an eccentric former Texas high school football coach would revolutionize football at a Division III college? Coach Mumme stayed with what he believed in and worked to be the best.
>
> Another game changer that comes to mind is Coach Eddie Robinson. I have met several of Coach Robinson's former players, and every one of them has told me about his unwavering commitment to coaching boys to championship men by keeping very high expectations. Coach Robinson made his players wear a coat and tie on trips, and to this day I know men in their forties and fifties who wear a coat and tie on casual Friday to honor Coach Robinson. Coach Robinson's high expectations, strong work ethic, and commitment to growing young men has made an unbelievable generational impact (Kevin Ozee, pers. comm.).

Family First Life's Shawn Meaike shares that those who most influenced him ranged from a parent to a kid his life intersected with only briefly while being hospitalized:

My mother taught me growing up the most about being a game changer. My mom was a single mom of two boys working three jobs. She told me that "in business and in sports everybody is always watching," and that "nobody has the right to judge you but God, but people will discern what you are all about." I believe game changers aren't worried about what other human beings think as long as what they are doing is in line with the Lord. My mother also taught me that my kindness would be mistaken as weakness and that most people aren't raised in strength—they will be looking to be led by strong people, and that leading people is a humbling experience to be cherished and not manipulated. Game changers understand their responsibility of being the first one on the battlefield and the last one off, and they relish it. They understand that their personal stuff can't be dumped on those they are charged with leading. Game changers also recognize that championships make them great players, not individual wins. If you can inspire people to believe in themselves and to achieve to the greatest of their ability, then you are a game changer.

Another major impression that stands out to me decades later happened when I was a nine-year-old. I was hit by a truck while riding my bicycle and I broke my arm, dislocated my hip, and had various other injuries. In the hospital bed next to me was a young boy named Kevin, and he had been hit and dragged under a car and received significant burns over a large portion of his body. I was getting out of the hospital much earlier than Kevin with a much better prognosis, and I remember I asked Kevin one day about this. He said he had nothing to complain about, and that it could be much worse. Not one day in the three weeks did I hear him complain. He was a pillar of strength that made me uncomfortable about complaining about my situation—so I didn't. Here was a young boy much worse off physically than I was who became a game changer in my life because he refused to whine, cry, or complain about his situation. When you lead people personally and professionally where there is zero self-pity and the utmost strength, you inspire greatness while removing self-doubt (Shawn Meaike, pers. comm.).

> It has been estimated that, on average, 155,000 people die each day on Earth. When you arise in the morning, your privilege and challenge are to validate why you are still here.

Sleeping with a Game Changer

Jeff Cowan, of Jeff Cowan's Pro Talk, explains how sometimes your game changer is your spouse, and that you can become a game changer for your spouse:

> I have learned that game changers cannot realize their full potential when they are not being led by game changers themselves. Although I had always prided myself on making Jeff Cowan's Pro Talk a game-changing company in the automotive service industry, I simply didn't achieve the height of my personal and professional success until I met the game changer in my life: my wife Candy.
>
> Maybe you think of game changers as being larger-than-life, iconic personalities, as the type of people who are revered by many or who have vast knowledge of the intricacies of the business world. Yet the fact is there is no typical game changer. It is different for everyone because every business and every situation is unique. Prior to meeting my wife Candy, I would rise each day and lug the stress of my early-morning e-mails, texts, and phone calls with me to work. I would anguish over the elements of running my business, and it would affect my attitude all day with my Pro Talk family.
>
> Over 70 percent of Pro Talk's business is generated on the East Coast. Since I live on the West Coast, my days begin at

5:00 AM. This early-morning start time gives me three hours each day before I arrive at the office to get a leg up on the challenges of the day. I use this time to organize my schedule and set my agenda. I collect my thoughts and focus my energy. Before Candy graced my life, I am afraid most days I failed in utilizing this time efficiently, and my business suffered.

Candy noticed that some mornings I was happy, enthusiastic, and highly energetic. However, she also noticed that, more times than not, morning saw me as stressed, having the wrong attitude, and being short-tempered and curt. This counter-productive mindset was directly a result of what was on the agenda for the day, and what I had seen or heard in my early-morning research. Candy can always assess my state of mind and help me to get refocused on what is important. She showed me the benefits of a positive attitude. Sure, before I met Candy, I had read and heard a million times that possessing a positive attitude is critical in business. I just could not see the flaw in myself. I thought I was doing everything right. It was Candy's mentoring that made me realize that the attitude that I set every morning is the one that I bring to work, and the one that sets the tone for every encounter I have that day. She made me understand that stress and negativity are draining and that I can be far more efficient if I approach the day with the "glass-half-full" perspective. I was wasting precious energy and time worrying and obsessing. The new approach with which she gifted me allows me to feel great about things, have a positive mindset, and pass that good energy on to my customers and employees.

The most important and perhaps most game-changing philosophy that Candy brought to me and that I now subscribe to is that when I am stressed about something, I either discuss what is causing the stress only with those directly involved or I don't discuss it at all. This was life-altering for me because it caused me to exercise great self-control. The time we make for our morning talks has made Candy my true game changer. In the past, I rarely noticed how I was behaving around others and how I was affecting them, good or bad. Now, each day, I have a clear picture of my state of mind and adjust it if necessary to ensure that it only affects the many game changers who work beside me at Pro Talk in the most positive and rewarding way. These morning conversations have become so important to me and Pro Talk that even when I travel and am away from home, I make time every morning to talk with Candy prior to starting my workday.

Candy is the type of person everyone loves. She has the world's biggest smile and she lights up the room. She sees only the positive in everyone and every situation. When she came into my life, it brought balance and a fresh perspective. She changed the game for me personally and professionally.

It is clear that game changers are a must in the workplace. But for me, and for many, I suspect, they see and understand there is a specific set of characteristics that a game changer must possess. Those characteristics will always be dictated by the need, the environment, and the challenges present. I have worked with top performers who were not what many would consider game changers, and I have worked with people who can't close a sale but who add an aspect to the office culture that makes everybody else perform at a higher level. That individual is a game changer and I will always want him or her on my team. You may not have to look very far or very hard to find your game changer. You do, however, have to open your mind as to where to find inspiration and motivation (Jeff Cowan, pers. comm.).

Don't Pave Detours to Destruction

Unfortunately, sometimes the people closest to you (coach, parent, and/or spouse) are a miserable influence. They are hypocrites who talk right and walk left. For example, the dad who grounds you for lying and then instructs you to tell Uncle Ralph on the phone that he's not in when he really is, or the business owner who preaches to "always do the right thing," then gives you a receipt for home improvements and tells you to list them as deductible business expenses. These influencers pave detours to destruction with their selfish and corrupt examples. Do not be one! And if you currently resemble the examples of deceit that were just given, *you* need to change, because I can assure you of this: When you end up missing your potential by a mile, and the sweat of your deathbed wakes you up to the fact that you blew it and missed your life, you will not have anyone else to blame for holding you back or stealing your dreams. Instead, you will be haunted by the fact that you could not get out of your own way. You stupidly and systematically self-destructed.

Hypocrisy Without Accountability at the Top

The Los Angeles Police Commission defines its purpose (as posted on its website) as follows:

> The Board of Police Commissioners, originally created in the 1920s, is comprised of five civilians who donate their time to the City while maintaining their professional careers. They are appointed by the Mayor and confirmed by the City Council. . . .
>
> The Commissioners' concerns are reflective of the community at large, and their priorities include implementing recommended reforms, improving service to the public by the Department, reducing crime and the fear of crime, and initiating, implementing, and supporting community policing programs.

On September 15, 2015, entertainment lawyer Matthew Johnson was elected president of the LAPD Police Commission after being appointed by Mayor Eric Garcetti. This high-profile opportunity to serve comes with the massive responsibility to set a stellar example, citywide, for respecting the law and advocating law enforcement integrity and accountability.

In May of 2017, President Johnson was captured in a TMZ video advocating the vandalizing of the President of the United States' Walk of Fame star on Hollywood Boulevard. His comments were then broadcast on TMZ's nationally televised show. That is an extreme version of leading by example—a reprehensible example. The police commission president's promotion of violence was a complete abdication of the commission's stated purpose, and diminished the entire police commission and every member on it. Johnson's irresponsible, immature, and hypocritical behavior has made law enforcement's job more difficult in protecting the public property he publicly favored trashing. He has created a mockery of his position as president of said commission, damaging any credibility he will need to hold law enforcement officials accountable for doing their jobs when he failed so miserably in his own duties to live out the commission's purpose and promote law and order.

You might think that a leader appointed to promote law and order, yet demonstrating hypocrisy through such a divisive and destructive example, would be removed from his position by the mayor who appointed him, but there were no consequences for Johnson's encouragement to destroy public property. In fact, Johnson's actions were offhandedly dismissed because he claims to have said them "in jest" and apologized for his actions. The example this sets for others is incredibly dangerous: that they can engage in such actions as encouraging violence, or hate speech, or racial slurs, or public bigotry, and the like, and then expect to suffer no consequences as long as they apologize and claim to have spoken in jest. The mayor also sets an egregious leadership example by holding a high-level leader he appointed to a lower standard than the average citizen would have endured had he or she publicly advocated violence. I contacted President Johnson, Mayor Garcetti, and the other four LAPD commission members for comment on Johnson's actions and none bothered to reply, which demonstrates another example: that of arrogance, or indifference, or both.

Let's quickly take a look back in the mirror: Just as President Johnson instantly demoted himself in the eyes of many from a leader to a clown, we are all prone to do likewise when we are unaware of just how compelling the power of our example is, for better or for worse, especially in our unguarded moments when we say things "in jest."

Game changers influence others with the power of their example. *What* the example is can either instill in others a desire to aspire or deliver disappointment and delusion. Take this responsibility seriously.

John, Zig, Johnny, and Harry

In our LearnToLead Elite Center near Los Angeles, where we conduct our Mission Unstoppable seminar, among others, throughout the year, I have a "wall of influence." I explain to our guests that the three men whose photos are posted on the wall are mentors who have had a significant positive impact on my life. They are, or were, game changers in their fields, and through my personal interaction with them my life was more completely equipped, stretched, and enhanced. These men are Dr. John C. Maxwell, who mentored me through his books and example in leadership; the late Zig Ziglar, who took an interest in me and helped me get my first book published; and my karate instructor, Master Johnny Gyro, who trained me to the rank of second-degree black belt. Businessman and philanthropist Harry Patterson is also a game changer for me; he gave me my first shot at a management position three decades ago. His is the classic story of a guy who started with nothing, built an automotive, real estate, and ranching empire, and now gives much of his time and fortune back to the less fortunate. People used to complain that Harry was hard to work for, but Harry Patterson was hard to work for only if you did not want to work! Harry was a great leader who expected a lot, but gave you the tools you needed to get there. We still stay in touch. He is the kind of friend who, if you were ever locked up in a foreign jail and held for ransom, he would bring lawyers, guns, and money to get you out; and if he couldn't get his hands on the lawyers, guns, and money soon enough, he would come by himself and figure it out on the fly.

The men on my wall of influence have not just made money; they have made a difference. They did not just become successful by crossing a finish line alone, but are significant because they brought so many others across that finish line with them. I am blessed to be one of them.

This raises the question: Whose wall of influence are you on? If you keep living with the example you are setting right now, whose wall of influence will you be on someday? Not everyone has a physical wall of influence, but there is a version in his or her mind and heart that treasures the relationship with someone who made a difference in his or her life. This is not because the person was easy on them, let them get by, or coddled them; rather, it is because he or she stretched them, equipped them, got in their face when they were off track, poured him- or herself into them, and left them better than he or she found them. If you have a mentor who is tough on you, thank him or her! Remember this:

- They are hard on you because they believe in you.
- They hold you accountable because they care.
- They stretch you so you never have to regret giving less than your best.
- They will not let you develop at your own pace, because your own pace is too safe, too slow, and too comfortable to take you to your potential.

Inheritance is what you leave behind. Legacy is whom you leave behind. Inheritance without legacy is evidence of a life lived selfishly, unfulfilled, and largely wasted.

Mission Unstoppable

To become an unstoppable game changer, consider and act on the following points:

1. Honestly evaluate the daily words, deeds, and attitude that constitute your example to those whom you care most about at home, at work, on the team, and in all your life's arenas:

- What about your example would make a great training film for aspiring game changers?
- What about your example would have to change *NOW* to make the film more compelling?

2. While you may have been given poor examples by parents, coaches, or bosses in the past, do you understand that *you* are still responsible for the example *you* choose to demonstrate daily, and that *you* have the power to choose to do better?

3. Enter each day with the objective to leave people better than you find them—whether they are serving you in a restaurant or on your team. How can you leave them more encouraged, equipped, clear, inspired, accepted, and valued than they were before your path crossed theirs? This is one of the most fulfilling aspects of living a game changer life.

4. Can you accept that before you can more effectively influence others, you must first change yourself (your thinking; your work ethic; your character; your WHY; the amount of time you spend in your zone; your attitude, passion, and enthusiasm; your personal philosophy; and the health of your mindset)? If you have not started already, will you start now?

5. Use additional and helpful resources to help yourself and others create game changer performance. Review behavioral expert Eric Samuelson's presentation in the Appendix at the conclusion of this book on how to use the Winslow Profiles to help you identify and develop game changers. At LearnToLead, we wouldn't think of bringing someone onto our team without this evaluation.

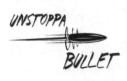

UNSTOPPA
BULLET

"This is the true joy in life, the being used for a purpose recognized by yourself as a mighty one; the being thoroughly worn out before you are thrown on the scrap heap; the being a force of Nature instead of a feverish selfish little clod of ailments and grievances complaining that the world will not devote itself to making you happy."—George Bernard Shaw (Shaw 1903, 29)

"I am of the opinion that my life belongs to the community, and as long as I live, it is my privilege to do for it whatever I can. I want to be thoroughly used up when I die, for the harder I work, the more I live. Life is no 'brief candle' to me. It is a sort of splendid torch which I have got hold of for a moment, and I want to make it burn as brightly as possible before handing it on to the future generations."—George Bernard Shaw (Goodreads 2017)

Epilogue

The late, legendary Tennessee Volunteers women's basketball coach Pat Summit, when sharing the influence of Coach Don Meyer on her life, made special mention of Coach Meyer's "Three Big Rules":

1. Everyone takes notes.
2. Everyone says please and thank you.
3. Everyone picks up the trash.

All three of these rules have both a literal and a mindset or mental application, and are simultaneously simple and profound. While all of the rules are significant and worth examining, I want to focus my final words of this book on the third rule. The literal application is obvious, of course: We should clean up after ourselves, respect our workspace, and pay attention to details. But the mental application is what is required for you to apply what you have learned in this book, and stick with it so that you can create the mindset and behaviors that will allow game changer status to dominate your life and make you become unstoppable.

"Everybody picks up the trash," in essence, says, "I will do whatever it takes to make this happen. I will start earlier, go later, and do more in between; there's no job or role beneath me during the process, and I will hold nothing back."

If you have followed through with each of the Mission Unstoppable exercises at the conclusions of the chapters in this book, then you have already started "picking up the trash"—doing whatever it takes—and it is essential that you leverage the momentum you have created.

However, if you skipped over them without taking action, both your sincerity and your commitment are in question. You have been entertained by this book, but nothing has really changed in your life as a result of what you have read in it. You are likely to continue your life as one of many, as just another ordinary head in a mediocre herd. Maybe you were looking for an easier way, or are not willing to give up your life of ease, or your excuses for what's held you back. Whatever. Here is just a thought, though: Before you go back to living your life talking like a big dog but walking like a pissant, before you persist in your shameful charade to become unstoppable, give this book to someone who is serious about changing his or her life. Heck, you will never miss it. All you did was *go through it*; you never *got from it*, anyhow. Your lack of action convicts you of complacency, so do the right thing and invest in someone who *will* do what is necessary to change his or her life. Fair enough?

However, if you have worked through the assignments and have begun assimilating the principles into your life, then you may have detected how each step reinforces the others—that there is a structured six-step process to follow to become unstoppable.

1. Once you clearly identify with what it is to be an unstoppable game changer, you have a specific standard to live up to each day.
2. Then, after you develop your WHY, you will naturally be more focused and more likely to stay in your zone.
3. Consequently, as you might expect, once your life has a clearer WHY and purpose, and you are more focused and in your zone daily, you will more consistently go A.P.E.—you will have a better attitude, more passion, and more enthusiasm. This, in turn, will augment your faith in the future and fuel more mental toughness for the journey.
4. As you then work to develop your personal philosophy, not only will you be in your zone more often, but your increased awareness will also nudge you to return faster if you depart.

5. Now it really gets good: With the ensuing surge of attitude, passion, enthusiasm, purpose, faith, and results, you will thirst for even more and leverage your momentum—leading you to developing a daily mindset discipline that renews your mind and transforms you, accelerating your results even further.

6. The big payoff is legacy, in that, as a natural result of your unstoppable mindset, behaviors, and results, you will make others wonder what you have, and inspire them to want what you have. This opens the door for you to have an impact on them with the power of your example, your knowledge, and your life.

And remember this: Becoming unstoppable is not a destination; it is a process. The day you think the journey is done is the day you begin to decline.

Enough said. Now go pick up the trash.

Appendix

The Winslow Profiles for Identifying and Developing Potential Game Changers

by Eric Samuelson

In this season of technological wonder, the prophetic lyrics to Paul Simon's terrific 1986 song, "The Boy in the Bubble," have entered the mainstream culture. Celebrity status has now been democratized. Every partially talented, wannabe playmaker is offered a chance at instant acclaim. One spectacular move, caught on camera, pushed, and retweeted to the excitement-addicted masses guarantees Andy Warhol's 15 minutes of fame to everyone. Thirty years ago, Simon and Warhol made independent, uncanny forecasts about our current culture. We are now living in the age they predicted.

Playmakers can actually look like principled game changers—for maybe a minute. The significant difference between the two is consistency. Who performs well even when the cameras are off? Who is willing to do the right thing simply because it's the right thing to do, regardless of the attention it garners? Who has the integrity to persevere? This is how character is tested and revealed.

Playmakers and game changers look an awful lot alike when they are in a peak-performance moment. Certainly there are some playmakers who can execute frequently enough that they *appear* to be game changers. They aren't actually displaying consistent peak performance, but have rather lucked into a series of successive opportunities that have allowed their massive skills to be publicly displayed.

Such moments can occur whether one is an NFL wide receiver, an eloquent politician, or a professional sales consultant.

We need to scratch the psychological surface with a well-constructed assessment to detect whether we're dealing with a predictable pro or a momentary hero. Skill is valuable, but it's not enough. The world is filled with skilled amateurs who can't sustain high performance. Here are three contrasts our firm uses to distinguish the playmaker from the game changer:

1. *Narcissism versus selflessness:* We market the powerful, deadly accurate Winslow Profiles to assist clients in hiring and development decisions. One vital trait we measure is "Conscientiousness." High scores here reflect a selfless, moral, duty-bound attitude. Individuals who score low operate from a self-centered "What's in it for me?" thought pattern. When low scores in this trait are clustered with low scores in "Nurturance" and "Recognition," we see a risk of narcissism. You can place a strong bet that an individual with low scores in those three traits is not an authentic game changer. Skill alone is not enough to overcome the selfish attitudes pervasive in such people.

2. *Miracles versus principles:* Playmakers live for the miraculous moment. They are comets that light up the sky for a minute. Game changers, however, operate by principles. These folks are analogous to the North Star—predictable and permanent enough to permit ship captains to steer to safe harbor. Game changers deduce the truths that govern consistent, productive value creation and then they operate by those deductions. First, we determine the qualities needed to live by such principles. We subsequently identify patterns to determine who is likely to live that way. Low scores in personality traits like "Endurance," "Coachability," "Responsibility," "Composure," and "(Self-)Control" inform coaches and executives which players are likely to operate by momentary miracles rather than principles.

3. *Transactions versus covenants:* The third quality of game changers is their view of commitments. These folks seem able to deliver what's asked, or they at least make valiant attempts to accomplish

what they promise. They refrain from indulging their passions or offering excuses. That alone is a strong, valuable quality. However, in some cases, game changers rise above mere commitment by forming and honoring *covenants*. This is a transcendent quality that pushes way past the conditional. A covenant takes relationship off the table.

To some the term *covenant* may seem antiquated. After all, in a no-fault divorce culture, we have reduced covenantal marriage to a matter of convenience and mood swings. So much of our lifestyle has deteriorated to momentary alignments. But certain game changers already operate beyond the momentary, pay-for-play culture. They make long-lasting, unbreakable attachments that rise above the mere exchange of value. They are way past deal making. There's certainly nothing wrong with transactions. When I want to buy a movie ticket, a sandwich, or my groceries, I'm probably not looking for a long-term relationship with the guy at the counter. But we are wise to distinguish the temporary financial transaction from the deep, ordained connections we have with certain key people. Playmakers need not apply for covenantal relationships. They are too busy doing deals in the green-room waiting for the cameras to roll. However, game changers who form covenants will at least have high scores in "Trust," "Contentment," and "Self-Confidence." We can reasonably connect with such folks in forming a solid, lasting bond where relationship is off the table.

It's encouraging to know that psychology and technology have now matured and merged to a point where the personality traits and behaviors of playmakers versus game changers are predictable to a very high degree of probability.

ERIC SAMUELSON is president of the Management Development Institute, a business consulting and personnel diagnostics service out of Richmond, Virginia. He has clients in 17 countries who rely on the incisive analysis offered by the Winslow Personality Assessment that he markets. He has seen both flash-in-the-pan, momentary, playmaker heroes and steady, reliable game changers. Each of these individuals has value at times, but it is vital for business executives to know the difference in advance. This highly validated psychometric tool allows Eric to offer rapid, accurate counsel to hundreds of decision makers. Because of the instrument's accuracy and objectivity, he is able to predict personnel behavior to a high degree of statistical accuracy. Eric can be reached at 804-798-3355 or eric@mdiworld.com.

References

Afremow, Jim. 2017. Twitter direct message to author, January 5.

Allen, James. 2015. *As a Man Thinketh*. Floyd, VA: Sublime Books.

AZ Quotes. 2017. Wind and Fly, LTD.

James Allen quotes. Accessed April 4, 2017. www.azquotes.com/quote/409998.

Georgio Armani quotes. Accessed March 24, 2017. www.azquotes.com/quote/10455.

Tony Blair quotes. Accessed April 13, 2017. www.azquotes.com/quote/28710.

Ken Blanchard quotes. Accessed March 30, 2017. www.azquotes.com/quote/29026.

David Brinkley quotes. Accessed April 6, 2017. www.azquotes.com/quote/36378.

Confucius quotes. Accessed April 17, 2017. www.azquotes.com/quote/62127.

Albert Einstein quotes. Accessed April 11, 2017. www.azquotes.com/quote/87313.

Viktor Frankl quotes. (a) Accessed April 4, 2017. www.azquotes.com/quote/101844; (b) Accessed April 4, 2017. www.azquotes.com/quote/101846; (c) Accessed April 5, 2017. www.azquotes.com/quote/461977.

Billy Graham quotes. Accessed April 13, 2017. www.azquotes.com/quote/797245.

William James quotes. (a) Accessed April 10, 2017. www.azquotes.com/quote/144844; (b) Accessed April 4, 2017. www.azquotes.com/quote/144848.

Helen Keller quotes. Accessed April 13, 2017. www.azquotes.com/quote/155007.

John F. Kennedy quotes. Accessed March 30, 2017. www.azquotes.com/quote/156190.

Bruce Lee quotes. www.azquotes.com/quote/171368.

Joe Louis quotes. www.azquotes.com/quote/603818.

Martin Luther King Jr. quotes. Accessed April 13, 2017. www.azquotes.com/quote/158971.

Vince Lombardi quotes. (a) Accessed April 10, 2017. www.azquotes.com/quote/178083; (b) Accessed April 4, 2017. www.azquotes.com/quote/178099.

John C. Maxwell quotes. www.azquotes.com/quote/539073.

Joel Osteen quotes. www.azquotes.com/quote/221738.

Norman Vincent Peale quotes. (a) Accessed April 14, 2017. www.azquotes.com/quote/227551; (b) Accessed April 13, 2017. www.azquotes.com/quote/1058001.

Jim Rohn quotes. Accessed March 30, 2017. (a) www.azquotes.com/quote/523792; (b) www.azquotes.com/quote/543435.

Bill Russell quotes. Accessed March 23, 2017. www.azquotes.com/quote/644541.

Albert Schweitzer quotes. Accessed April 18, 2017. www.azquotes.com/quote/263174.

Henry David Thoreau quotes. Accessed April 14, 2017. www.azquotes.com/quote/294027.

Leo Tolstoy quotes. www.azquotes.com/quote/295490.

Azem, Samar. 2017. E-mail message to author. March 1.

Barnette, Dan. 2017. E-mail message to author. April 8.

Bartlett, Brad. 2017. E-mail message to author. March 27.

Bastian, Ed. 2017. E-mail message to author. March 28.

Beckner, Phil. 2017. E-mail message to author. January 5.

Bible Gateway. 2017. Holy Bible. New King James Version. 2 Corinthians 5:7. Accessed April 13, 2017. https://www.biblegateway.com/passage/?search=2+Corinthians+5%3A7& version=NKJV.

Matthew 25:23. Accessed March 23, 2017.
https://www.biblegateway.com/passage/?search=Matthew+25%3A23& version=NLT.

Biblica. 2017. Holy Bible. New International Version.
John 15:13. Accessed April 12, 2017. www.biblica.com/bible/online-bible/?action=bible_widget_refresh&translation=niv&book=john&chapter=15.
Luke 17:10. Accessed March 22, 2017. www.biblica.com/bible/online-bible/?action=bible_widget_refresh&translation=niv&book=luke&chapter=17.
Proverbs 29:15. Accessed April 26, 2017. www.biblica.com/bible/online-bible/?action=bible_widget_refresh&translation=niv&book=proverbs&chapter=29.
Romans 12:2. Accessed April 14, 2017. www.biblica.com/bible/online-bible/?action=bible_widget_refresh&translation=niv&book=romans&chapter=12.

Breathnach, Sarah Ban. 1996. *The Simple Abundance Journal of Gratitude*. New York: Warner Books.

Carter, Doug. 2017. E-mail message to author. April 8.

Cowan, Jeff. 2017. E-mail message to author. February 28.

Crean, Tom. 2017. Phone conversation with author. April 12.

Cross, Scott. 2017. E-mail message to author. January 5.

Dettmann, Andrew. 2017. E-mail message to author. April 17.

Dictionary.com. 2017. "Mediocre." www.dictionary.com/browse/mediocre. Accessed April 24, 2017.

Dorfman, Larry. 2017. E-mail message to author. February 19.

Englen, Bjorn. 2017. E-mail message to author. March 1.

Ferrell, Yogi. 2017. Phone conversation with author. April 10.

Forrester, Robert. 2017. E-mail message to author. January 7.

Goodreads. 2017. "A Quote by George Bernard Shaw." Accessed April 18, 2017.
www.goodreads.com/quotes/456466-i-am-of-the-opinion-that-my-life-belongs-to.

Google. 2017.

"Attitude Definition." Accessed April 11, 2017.
https://www.google.com/search?q=attitude+definition&oq=
attitude+definition&aqs=chrome.0.69i59.3407j0j7&sourceid
=chrome&ie=UTF-8.

"Energy Definition." Accessed April 4, 2017.
https://www.google.com/search?q=energy&oq=energy&aqs
=chrome.0.69i59l2.1343j0j7&sourceid=chrome&ie=UTF-8.

"Enthusiasm Definition." Accessed April 12, 2017.
https://www.google.com/search?q=enthusiasm+definition&oq
=enthu&aqs=chrome.0.69i59l2j69i57j69i60.1031j0j7
&sourceid=chrome&ie=UTF-8.

"Faith Definition." Accessed April 13, 2017.
https://www.google.com/search?q=faith+definition&oq=faith
+de&aqs=chrome.0.69i59j69i57.1487j0j4&sourceid=chrome
&ie=UTF-8.

"Lazy Definition." Accessed April 24, 2017.
https://www.google.com/search?q=lazy&oq=lazy&aqs=
chrome.69i57j69i59.639j0j4&sourceid=chrome&ie=UTF-8.

"Mindset Definition." Accessed April 17, 2017.
https://www.google.com/search?q=mindset+definition&oq
=mindset+&aqs=chrome.1.69i57j69i59j69i61l2.1903j0j4
&sourceid=chrome&ie=UTF-8.

"Relentless definition." Accessed March 20, 2017.
https://www.google.com/search?q=relentless+definition
&oq=relent&aqs=chrome.1.69i59l3j69i57j69i60l2.1599j0j7
&sourceid=chrome&ie=UTF-8#dobs=relentless.

Gyro, Johnny. 2017. E-mail message to author. March 7.

Hermann, Adam. 2017. E-mail message to author. January 20.

Janssen, Jeff. 2017. E-mail message to author. February 21.

Klintworth, Mike. 2017. E-mail message to author. April 4.

Leonard, Meyers. 2017. Text message with author. 2017.

Loscalzo, Jason. 2017. E-mail message to author. February 15.

Malishenko, John. 2017. E-mail message to author. March 16.

Maroney, Oliver. 2017. Twitter direct message to author. January 6.

Maxwell, John C. 2005. *Developing the Leader Within You*. Nashville, TN: Thomas Nelson Inc.

Maxwell, John C. 2006. *The Difference Maker: Making Your Attitude Your Greatest Asset*. Nashville, TN: Thomas Nelson Inc.

McCaw, Allistair. 2017. E-mail message to author. January 25.

Meaike, Shawn. 2017. E-mail message to author. March 9.

Merriam-Webster. 2017. *Merriam-Webster Learner's Dictionary*. "Momentum." Accessed April 24, 2017. https://www.merriam-webster.com/dictionary/momentum.
"Passion." Accessed April 11, 2017.
www.learnersdictionary.com/definition/passion.

Mills, Marisa. 2017. E-mail message to author. February 3.

Ozee, Kevin. 2017. E-mail message to author. March 2.

Palka, Cory. 2017. E-mail message to author. March 2.

Quoteland. 2017. John Wesley quotes. Accessed April 12, 2017. www.quoteland.com/rate/John-Wesley-Quotes/49854/.

Ram, Alan. 2017. E-mail message to author. March 5.

Ramonat, Whit. 2017. E-mail message to author. January 8.

Rohn, Jim. 1999. *The Weekend Seminar*. Jim Rohn International. DVD.

Samuelson, Eric. 2017. E-mail message to author. April 18.

Shaw, Bernard. 1903. *Man and Superman*. Cambridge, MA: The University Press; Bartleby.com, 1999. Accessed April 18, 2017. www.bartleby.com/157/.

Tomlinson, Troy. 2017. E-mail message to author. January 19.

Wikipedia contributors. 2017. *Wikipedia, The Free Encyclopedia*. "Mental toughness." Accessed April 13, 2017.
https://en.wikipedia.org/w/index.php?title=Mental_toughness&oldid=760275543.
"Yogi Ferrell." Accessed April 17, 2017.
https://en.wikipedia.org/w/index.php?title=Yogi_Ferrell&oldid=775348743.

Williams, David. 2017. E-mail message to author. January 7.

Wilson, Dave. 2017. E-mail message to author. April 1.

Index

Bring Dave to Your Team

 Book Dave to come in-house and get your entire team on the same page at the same time. Dave's private engagements range from one-hour keynote speeches for kickoff meetings, dinners, retreats, or conventions to half-day/full-day/multiday seminars with your team.

For more information on our wide array of sales and leadership topics, customized pricing, and available dates, please contact Rhonda at 818-735-9503 or e-mail Rhonda@learntolead.com.